# LEADING BLIND
# WITHOUT VISION

# LEADING BLIND WITHOUT VISION

## THE BENEFITS OF HIRING THE BLIND AND VISUALLY IMPAIRED

WELBY BROADDUS

NEW DEGREE PRESS

LEADING BLIND WITHOUT VISION
*The Benefits of Hiring the Blind and Visually Impaired*

| ISBN | 978-1-63730-846-2 | *Paperback* |
| | 978-1-63730-912-4 | *Kindle Ebook* |
| | 978-1-63730-940-7 | *Ebook* |

*This book is dedicated to my son, Welby Tre'Vaughn Broaddus. The day you were born, you inspired me to always put my best foot forward. I've always wanted to be your role model to show you the rewards you receive from putting in hard work to ensure that your dreams come true. You are a wonderful person, and I love you, son.*

*Even though they are not with us anymore, I want to also dedicate my book to my grandparents. I have had the pleasure of knowing all of my grandparents and learning lifelong lessons from all of them. Thank you, Lessie M. Kidd, Nannie R. Broaddus, Ruby M. Kidd, Sylvester T. Kidd, and Welby B. Broaddus.*

# CONTENTS

---

# INTRODUCTION

---

David Hunt is a blind winemaker and owner of Hunt Cellars. For over twenty years, Hunt has made wines that have won best in-class awards and been enjoyed by thousands all over the world. Hunt's success illustrates that it is not what you can't do, but what you can.

Hunt said that his secret to success came down to courage. "People with handicaps don't have to do the 'poor me.' They just gotta go out and do it." Hunt has said that "Everybody is two people. The person they are and the person they want to become. Most people never pursue that second one because negativity sets in. They live on the margins. They focus on why they can't do it. But all you need is one reason why you can do it: because you love it" (Alimurung, 2013).

David Hunt's story is not uncommon in the business world and there are many stories just like his. Hunt is a great example of why the blind and visually impaired (BVI) are just as capable as sighted people on the job and in business. Too often when a hiring manager or recruiter meets someone who is BVI, there is a stigma that the individual has more limitations to their capabilities than just their sight.

## THE PROBLEM

The average unemployment rate for individuals who are BVI is 70 percent. A lot of hiring managers feel that there are not many jobs at their companies that an employee who is BVI can accomplish. They believe that it would be expensive to provide the appropriate equipment to accommodate an employee who is BVI. They would need someone to assist them in performing their job duties, and the managers feel that employees who are BVI are more prone to work related injuries.

People with disabilities have always found obtaining employment challenging. Before the Industrial Revolution, the only jobs that were available for people who were BVI were jobs that did not require physical capabilities like a tailor, silver and goldsmith, shoemaker, or cook. Even these jobs were not easily obtainable because they required an assistant to identify colors and objects.

During the industrial revolution, many jobs were created in sweatshops for the immigrants that came to the United States. There was so much competition among job seekers who did not have a disability during this time that many employers did not give people with disabilities employment opportunities. This was perfectly legal, for there were not any government acts that required employers to hire people with disabilities.

Once the Americans with Disabilities Act (ADA) passed in 1990, there were more employment opportunities for people who are BVI. This was also the start of the United States offering federal jobs to people with disabilities. In 1996, the

Telecommunications Act became law and required that telecommunications manufacturers and service providers were
equipped to be accessible to people with disabilities.

## THE REALITY

With the advancement of technology and adaptation devices
like screen reading, magnifying software, braille terminals,
and many other tools, employees who are BVI can work in
almost any field.

According to Belo Miguel Cipriani, "the reality is that a blind
person can do any job that involves a computer and there are
a slew of adaptive tech toys that make most jobs accessible
such as a portable scanner to read printed material. As for the
purported expense, according to the American Foundation
for the Blind, most accommodations cost less than $1,000, a
negligible amount for a serious business." According to the
Virginia Commonwealth University, Rehabilitation Research
& Training Center (VCU-RRTC), employees with disabilities
have the same absentee and sick rates as employees who do
not have a disability. Employees with disabilities are average or above average when it comes to performance, quality
and quantity of work, flexibility to demands, attendance,
and safety.

Employers should start thinking outside of the box when
it comes to their hiring practices, for the BVI community
is an untargeted employee pool. They are natural problem
solvers, for they must have a creative personality to manage
their disability on a daily basis.

If you want to continue to be pertinent as an employer with good hiring practices, establishing a work environment of inclusivity for employees who are BVI is important. Everyone in the organization benefits from a diverse work environment. Employees that do not have a disability will become more attentive in maintaining an inclusive and accessible work area. The employees that are BVI will be able to share a different perspective when it comes to creativity and problem-solving that the sighted employees may have not considered. Also, businesses that employ people who are BVI bring in higher profits. A 2018 report by Accenture and the American Association of People with Disabilities on Business.com shows that businesses that target individuals with disabilities have a 30 percent higher profit margin than businesses that do not target this population.

## MY STORY

At birth, I was diagnosed with optic atrophy and nystagmus. Optic atrophy is a condition that affects the optic nerve, and nystagmus is an eye condition where the eyes make repetitive, uncontrollable movements.

In 1985, I was a senior attending Akron Buchtel High School. The seniors were meeting with our guidance counselor. She wanted to assist us in mapping out our career path after graduation. At this point in my life, I was finally feeling less insecure about my visual impairment. I felt good about what I wanted to do with myself after high school until I received the call slip to go meet with my counselor. I do not remember everything we talked about that day, but I do remember the conversation we had when she asked me what my plans were after graduation. I informed her that I planned to attend either Kent State University or Akron University, which is now the University of Akron. I planned on majoring in Computer Science. She told me with no hesitation that college is not for me. I should try to find a job. From that day forward, her remarks fueled my desire to go to college and graduate.

I left her office devastated and angry because she never took the time to help or get to know me as a visually impaired student. I was attending a traditional school without any assistance and overcoming the daily challenges of regular high school in addition to the challenges I was facing as a legally blind student.

That statement inspired me to earn two degrees and to become the person I am now. Today, I have over ten years of experience as a career specialist, teaching at-risk youth, adults, and individuals with disabilities employable skills. Every day I helped this country's future leaders obtain employment, enroll in college, or enlist into the military.

In my current position as a Misdemeanor Case Manager at Summit County Juvenile Court in Akron, Ohio, I meet with youth and families to explain the court process, address any questions, and provide them with any pertinent documentation they will need. I also attend court hearings with the youth and families. I have been employed with the court for ten years.

I am also a small business owner and the founder of Broaddus Business Solutions, where I help entrepreneurs and small business owners register their business with the Secretary of

State Office, create marketing and business plans, and provide one-on-one consulting sessions. I've seen both sides of the issue and understand the challenges companies face in hiring people who are BVI.

## A VISION OF THE FUTURE

In May of 2002, VCU-RRTC conducted a national research study of employer's experiences of employees with disabilities. The results of the study showed that employees with disabilities can be productive as it relates to timeliness, punctuality, task consistency, and work speed.

This book has been on my mind for many years. I knew that someone had to share the stories about the positive qualities that people who are BVI bring to an organization. Employers sometimes have difficulty addressing or accommodating us. Their intentions are good, but their actions can come across as unempathetic. Often this comes from a simple misunderstanding about how to communicate, identify, and address the needs of the applicants or employees who are BVI. We've all been there.

There was a time when I was working as a Career Specialist at one of the high schools here in Akron. One of my very outgoing students was not being her jovial self. This went on for a couple of weeks, so I decided to check in on her to see what was going on. One morning, I was walking down the hall and she was standing at her locker. I walked over to her. I did not want to just come over and start playing twenty questions, so I began asking, "How are you doing?"

She responded, "I am doing fine," in a somber tone. I stood there for a little while making small talk with her when I decided to ask the question.

"Are you pregnant?"

She looked at me and shouted out, "Oh my god!" and slammed her locker door and walked off very fast. I felt so bad for even asking the question. Moreover, she did not talk to me for about a month.

As time passed and I thought about my approach, I realized that I should have handled the matter a totally different way. I could have approached her and expressed that I noticed that she has not been her happy-go-lucky self lately and let her know that I am here for her if she needed someone to talk to. There were other counselors in the building that specifically deal with these types of situations. I should have reached out to one of these professionals beforehand. They could have advised me on the best approach to take, or they could have reached out to the student themselves.

The lesson here is that just as I could have handled the situation with my student differently, employers can use the same philosophy with their employees who are BVI. Through communication and well-established partnerships with resource agencies, they can employ the applicants that are BVI and address any matters related to inclusivity.

After reading this book, I want you to have a better understanding of how exceptional the BVI community really is. I want you to know that when you meet someone who is BVI, you're most likely encountering someone that has sharpened their senses and abilities in ways unrelated to vision. It's these skill sets, such as adaptability, dedication, creativity, motivation, and memory that make them valuable assets to any company in any industry.

*Leading Blind without Vision: The Benefits of Hiring the Blind and Visually Impaired* is a resource for business owners, executives, and HR professionals to learn how to accommodate the BVI community, learn about the skills that they use every day that are transferable into the work environment, and identify ways to ensure that their employees that are BVI have a positive experience within their organizations.

# PART I

# THE PAST,
# THE PRESENT,
# AND
# THE FUTURE
# OF BLIND
# AND VISUALLY
# IMPAIRED
# WORK

# CHAPTER 1

# HISTORY OF DISCRIMINATION AGAINST THE BLIND AND VISUALLY IMPAIRED

———

## TIMELINE OF PROGRESS

The term "disability" was first coined sometime between 1861 and 1865 for the soldiers that were injured during the Civil War. The Civil War Pension laws allowed for Union Army veterans who were disabled from the war and unable to perform manual labor jobs to receive pensions. They defined a disability as an infirmity that precluded equal participation in society and the ability to earn an independent living (Blanck 2008).

Over the years, society has viewed people with disabilities as deformed and unable to participate in society (Blanck 2008). The disability could be a mental or physical condition that was acquired at birth or from injury or illness.

In the '60s, The United States government expanded the Social Security entitlement program to provide medical assistance for those individuals living in poverty and those who have a disability (Blanck 2008). This program did not address the segregation of people with disabilities from employment, housing, and education. People with disabilities were still denied access to retail establishments, restrooms, and public transportation. Qualified individuals could not enter the workforce because there was no accessible work environment for potential employees with a disability. Employers also discriminated against potential job candidates that were disabled.

During this time, the civil rights movement was taking form, and this created the opportunity for disability activists to fight for the rights of people with disabilities. These groups would not only fight for the disabled but also minority groups in search of equal rights, opportunities, and fair treatment (Anti-Defamation League 2021).

Parents of children with disabilities played a major role in the progress of the movement over the years. Along with disability rights activist, they lobbied the government for legislation to combat the social and physical barriers that people with disabilities had to deal with, and they wanted children with disabilities to be removed from institutions and placed into schools so they could be able to interact within society just as children without a disability could (Anti-Defamation League 2021).

In 1962, The President's Committee on Employment of the Physically Handicapped was renamed the President's Committee on Employment of the Handicapped and the focus was on employment issues that affected people with cognitive disabilities and mental illness (Kansas Council on Developmental Disabilities 2021). The same year, Edward Roberts sued The University of California, Berkeley, to become the first student with a wheelchair to attend the university (Leon 2021).

In 1963, President John F. Kennedy called for a reduction in residential institutions which resulted in deinstitutionalization and increased community services (Kansas Council on Developmental Disabilities 2021).

In 1965, The Vocational Rehabilitation Amendments of 1965 were passed. This authorized that federal money be allocated for the construction of rehabilitation centers, the expansion of existing vocational rehabilitation programs, and the creation of the National Commission on Architectural Barriers to Rehabilitation of the Handicapped (Tiner 2018). In that same year, The Voting Rights Act of 1965 became law. This allowed for the protection for minority voting rights. It also permitted individuals with disabilities to have assistance in voting (US Department of Justice 2014).

During the '70s, people with disabilities started viewing themselves as minorities just like any other minority group in the United States. They wanted the same protections that other minority groups were receiving, so they marched on Washington and lobbied Congress to get their own civil rights language for people with disabilities in the 1972 Rehabilitation Act, which became law in 1973 (Anti-Defamation League 2021). "Some people may have thought it was undignified for people in wheelchairs to crawl in that manner, but

I felt that it was necessary to show the country what kinds of things people with disabilities have to face on a day-to-day basis. We had to be willing to fight for what we believed in," said Michael Winter (Meldon, 2019). This gave this population civil rights protections for the first time. Through protesting, people with disabilities got laws passed that guaranteed accessibility to employment, voting, air travel, and independence in housing and education.

Section 504 of The Rehabilitation Act of 1973 gave people with disabilities equal employment opportunity within the federal government and federally funded programs. The act prohibits discrimination on the basis of physical or mental disability. This section also established the Architectural and Transportation Barriers Compliance Board. They are responsible for mandating equal access to public services to people with disabilities. An example of these services are public transportation services and housing. The Architectural and Transportation Barriers Compliance Board are responsible for the distribution of funds for vocational training as well (Anti-Defamation League 2021).

In 1975, the Education for All Handicapped Children Act was passed into law, which guaranteed equal access to public education for children with disabilities. This act indicates that every child has a right to education and mandates the inclusion of children with disabilities in conventional education classrooms. The only reason that this does not apply is if the satisfactory level of education could not be accomplished because of the essence of the students' disability. In 1990, the Education for All Handicapped Children Act name was changed to the Individuals with Disabilities Education Act

(IDEA). The act still focused on the inclusion of children with disabilities into the regular classroom setting. The act also included the rights of parents to be involved in the educational decisions that affect their child. IDEA specifies that a child's Individual Education Plan (IEP) must have parental approval to meet the educational needs of a student with a disability (Anti-Defamation League 2021). During high school, Dr. Mona Minkara's IDEA rights were almost denied.

Dr. Mona Minkara, a tenure-track Assistant Professor of Bioengineering and Affiliated Faculty of Chemistry and Chemical Biology at Northeastern University in Boston, MA, sat down with me for an interview. During my interview with Minkara, she told me she was diagnosed with macular degeneration and cone-rod dystrophy. Macular degeneration occurs when the central portion of the retina deteriorates (American Macular Degeneration Foundation 2017). Cone-rod dystrophy is a group of similar eye conditions that causes the loss of vision (US National Library of Medicine 2020). Minkara shared an experience that she had in school when one of her teachers wanted to stop her from taking an Advanced Placement (AP) class.

She said, "I remember recognizing as a kid that the education quality was lower in the lower classes, and those were the classes that I was in." While sitting in her seventh-grade science class, Minkara realized that it was time for a change after arguing with her teacher over a science experiment. "I remember getting into an argument with my seventh grade teacher because she was telling us that ice is denser than liquid water," says Minkara. She never knew her potential during school, but she did recognize that she was bored.

During her tenth grade year, Minkara decided to go speak with the teacher who was the head of the science department and taught the AP Biology class about getting permission to be scheduled in her class. She said, "I was bored out my mind, so how much worse could it get?" When she approached the teacher to ask her if she would allow her to take the class, the teacher was not supportive or encouraging.

The teacher said, "You will fail. You do not belong in my class, and I am not going to modify my teaching for you." Minkara was granted permission to take the class, and she ended up receiving one of the highest grades. After the class was over, the teacher approached Minkara to apologize for her actions. Getting one of the highest grades in the class really boosted Minkara's confidence to enroll into other AP classes.

"If I can do that, then I probably can do other things," says Minkara. She believes that everyone should be given the opportunity to try different things. She goes on to say, "No one knows everything about their future. You don't know if you can do anything until you try."

Even though many amendments and acts passed for the rights of people with disabilities, there was still a lot of work to be done.

During the 1980s, advocates for people with disabilities were lobbying and campaigning for different pieces of legislation that relates to people with disabilities to be protected under one civil rights statue. They wanted it to be similar to the 1964 Civil Rights Act, which prohibited discrimination on the basis of race, religion, national origin, or gender (Anti-Defamation League 2021).

On July 26, 1990, the Americans with Disabilities Act (ADA) was signed into law by President George H. W. Bush. This act prohibits discrimination on the basis of disability in employment, state and local government, public accommodations, commercial facilities, transportation, and telecommunications.

Their advocacy paid off. In the next chapter, we will talk about the Americans with Disabilities Act (ADA) which was passed into law in 1990. Without this act, I would not have become the person that I am today. I would not have been given the many opportunities to be employed with the various jobs I have worked over the years. If I was employed, more than likely I would not have longevity with my employers due to the accommodations I need to perform jobs successfully. When riding public transportation, I would have been expected to navigate through the system without any assistance. To be perfectly frank, you would not be reading this book right now if the ADA guidelines were not passed into law, since I am a visually impaired author.

---

**THE BOTTOM LINE**
- In 1965, The Vocational Rehabilitation Amendments of 1965 were passed, authorizing federal money to be allocated for the construction of rehabilitation centers.

- In 1975, the Education for All Handicapped Children Act was passed which guaranteed equal access to public education for children with disabilities.
- On July 26, 1990, the Americans with Disabilities Act (ADA) was signed into law, prohibiting discrimination on the basis of disability in employment, state and local government, public accommodations, commercial facilities, transportation, and telecommunications.

# CHAPTER 2

# A PERSISTENT ISSUE: THREE CASES OF MODERN DISCRIMINATION

Title One of the ADA applies to employment, and it requires employers with fifteen or more employees to provide qualified individuals with disabilities an equal opportunity to benefit from the full range of employment opportunities available to others (US Department of Justice 2020). This means employers are not allowed to discriminate against a person with a disability when it comes to recruitment, hiring and promoting, training, salary, social activities, and other benefits that comes along with employment. The employer is prohibited to ask the applicant about his or her disability before offering them the job. They are required to make reasonable accommodations to the known disability of the new hires, unless it results in undue hardship (US Department of Justice 2020). An undue hardship is defined as being an action that requires considerable difficulty or is expensive to provide (ADA National Network 2021). A large employer with many resources would be expected to make more accommodations than a smaller employer with very little or limited resources. Undue hardship is evaluated on a case-by-case basis.

## HEAD CHEF TO KITCHEN AID

Brian Banks is a fifty-six-year-old retired chef who lost his vision as an adult. Banks is considered to be legally blind due to a detached retina, which leaves him completely blind in one eye and with partial vision in the other. During an interview with Banks, he told me about his experience working for a small Christian academy where he worked as head chef. He was responsible for preparing and serving the meals for the school's breakfast and lunch programs. This was a small Christian school that did not have many students.

The school decided to participate in Ohio's private school voucher program. This is a program that allows students from kindergarten through high school to receive EdChoice scholarships to pay for private school tuition if they are students from low-income families or their home public school is identified as underperforming (Kelley 2020). Since the school decided to accept EdChoice scholarships, they felt that they needed to hire another cafeteria worker to assist Banks with the breakfast and lunch program. However, that was not the real reason. The school was worried about what parents would think about their children's lunches being prepared by a person who is blind. "They were worried about me knowing how to cook the children's food. Do I know the difference if I put salt or sugar in something," said Banks. Once they brought on another person to assist Banks, his responsibilities were gradually taken away. Banks said, "What they really did was bring in somebody to take over." His employer did not inform him that he was being replaced. They just reduced his duties. "They didn't just say 'well, we have to let you go.' They actually reduced me from being the man running the kitchen to the guy pouring milk," Banks said.

Banks decided to go talk with the principal about how things were being handled. Banks said to the principal, "Listen, if you had a problem with me, then you just should have come and explained it to me. But the way that you did it, I didn't agree with." Mr. Banks informed the principal that he has the credentials to be a chef and that is what he was trained and certified to do. It really bothered him how the school administration treated him. "They made my position so insignificant that I had to just walk away," said Banks.

The job became so unbearable that he decided to quit. Since the school was a small Christian school, he did not want to bring attention to how the administration treated its employees with disabilities. Also, Banks's children were attending the school at the time, and he did not want them to be mistreated if he filed a discrimination claim against the school.

According to the American Foundation for the Blind in 2017, the employment rate for blind and visually impaired employees was 44 percent compared to 79 percent for non-disabled employees. The unemployment rate for workers who do not have a disability fluctuates up and down over time based on what is going on in the economy. When the economy is good, the unemployment rates are lower and when it is bad, the rates is higher. The average unemployment rate for the employees who are BVI is 70 percent all the time. One of the factors that contributes to such a high unemployment rate for BVI community is discriminatory practices of employers. The ADA prohibits discrimination against employees with disabilities, but it is still happening. Discrimination is one of the biggest barriers to employment for the job seeker who is BVI (Myers 2016).

## AN UNNECESSARY TEST

On June 10, 2020, Disability Rights Advocates (DRA), a non-profit disability rights legal center that advances the rights and opportunities for people with disabilities throughout the United States, posted on their website that they filed a discrimination charge with the Equal Employment Opportunity Commission (EEOC) against the state of New York on behalf of Matthew Herrera. The EEOC website says that they were established in 1965 to be responsible for enforcing federal laws that make it illegal to discriminate against any job applicant or employee because of their race, color, religion, sex, national origin, age, disability, or genetic information. DRA felt that the state of New York had discriminated against Herrera because he is visually impaired. Herrera applied for a position of Mental Health Therapy Aide Trainee (MHTAT) at a New York City mental health clinic.

"In early April 2019, I learned of a Spanish language MHTAT position at the Audubon Clinic, an outpatient mental health clinic located in the Washington Heights neighborhood of New York City," said Herrera. He is diagnosed with bilateral retinal detachment. The Mayo Clinic defines this as a serious eye condition that occurs when the retina pulls away from the blood vessels that provides it with oxygen and nutrients. After failing the state's bright-line rule, which disqualifies an applicant whose binocular vision is lower than 20/40 from being employed, Herrera was disqualified for the position of MHTAT.

DRA and Herrera believe that the policy does not have any connection with the MHTAT's responsibilities that he would be required to perform. He said, "I saw a job description for the MHTAT position. It was similar to the one currently posted on the Department of Civil Service's website, which states MHTATs provide direct services, treatment, rehabilitation, and support to individuals diagnosed with mental illness. They . . . help individuals to participate in games and recreational programs; coach and encourage individuals to develop daily living skills; and provide a clean, safe, and comfortable environment." It prevents qualified people with disabilities from getting an equal chance to show that they are capable of completing the job requirements (DRALegal. org 2020).

Mr. Herrera's case with the EEOC is still an active case. He is sure that he is capable of performing the job as a MHTAT based on his previous work experience. "For the past eight years, I have worked in the fields of security and mental health services. I have never asked an employer for any reasonable accommodation related to my vision before, and I have never received any accommodation to successfully do my job," said Herrera (DRALegal.org 2020).

The interview of a person who has a disability should be conducted in the same manner as a person who does not. The interviewer should keep the focus of the conversation on how the interviewee can carry out job duties.

## ASKING THE RIGHT QUESTIONS

"I made a decision that I was going to be upfront about my disability from day one. It's all over my application; my needs are clearly outlined. I just didn't want to end up in an institution that didn't really want to work with me," said Dr. Mona Minkara. She had a lot of job offers and several interviews after receiving her postdoctorate from the University of Florida in 2015. When she began applying for faculty positions all over the country, Minkara decided to be upfront about her blindness and needs. After being transparent about her condition and what she would need from the potential employer to perform the duties that would be required of her, she still was discriminated against during one of her interviews.

Minkara was invited to this particular university for a faculty interview. She would like the university to remain anonymous. She describes the process of a faculty interview as two days of meeting after meeting.

"The way the process goes for faculty interviews is that it's two days of grilling and meeting after meeting. You are meeting everybody in the department, the dean, and I don't know who else. It's just a lot of people," said Minkara. She was really excited about the possibility of being employed with this university until she sat down to meet with the chair of the hiring committee.

When she walked into the chair's office to meet with him, he was an older gentleman and was very direct in his conversation. His first words to Minkara were, "So, I see that you are blind."

This threw Minkara off-guard for a moment because she was not expecting anyone to ask her that type of question during an interview, but she responded "yes."

The chair continued, "Well, how do you do this job?" As Minkara began to explain how she was qualified and the ways she would go about completing the duties of the job, the chair cut her off mid-sentence and said, "I don't think you can do this job."

Minkara responded, "Why did you fly me out here for this interview?"

The chair said, "I think we made a mistake."

Minkara was at a loss for words at this point. She said, "Okay."

Minkara knew that she was being discriminated against. "I answered all of his questions even though I had learned that employers have no right in a job interview to mention my disability. They can only ask how I do my job," said Minkara. She really had a problem with the chair focusing on her disability instead of the contributions Minkara could bring to the university.

After her encounter with the chair of the hiring committee, she returned to meet with the dean of the department. She asked Minkara, "How was your visit?"

Minkara explained to the dean what happened. Minkara informed the dean that the conversation with the chair really changed her mind about wanting to become a part of her staff. Minkara said, "This one interaction really dampened my mood because I was excited about this job prospect." Shortly after, Minkara informed the dean about her interview with the chair, the university forced him to retire, as he had received a lot of similar complaints in the past. Minkara said, "I was the straw that broke the camel's back."

---

**THE BOTTOM LINE**
- The BVI's struggle for equal rights has been long and arduous. Through a deeper understanding on the history of people with disabilities, you can become an advocate for a better tomorrow.
- Learn about the ADA guidelines; they will assist you in identifying the best practices for hiring and employing the BVI community.
- Adopt ADA employment guidelines into your business's employment philosophy to become more inclusive. Prevent businesses' discrimination in the workplace and create a brand for an inclusive society.

## CHAPTER 3

# WHY NOW: THE POWER OF TECHNOLOGY

---

### THE EVOLUTION OF TECHNOLOGY

Assistive technology has come a long way since I started receiving those type of items from the Visual Service for the Visually Impaired (VSVI). I used talking books, large print books, computers with large monitors, handheld magnifiers, electronic video magnifier, and ZoomText.

When I first began receiving services from VSVI in the seventh grade, one of the first pieces of accessibility technology that I received were talking books. They were introduced to society and sponsored by the Library of Congress in 1933 (VisionAware.org 2020). These are books that are recorded on vinyl records. These records were created to provide verbalized recordings for individuals who were blind and visually impaired (BVI). Later on down the road, these same vinyl records became more popular when they were used to record music (VisionAware.org 2020). They were pretty cool; you played the talking book on a phonograph, also known as a record player. This is an instrument used for reproducing sound by the vibration of a stylus or needle that follows a groove on the vinyl record as it rotates on the record player (Britannica.com 2019).

I remember being pretty excited about receiving talking books and a record player to listen to the stories. The record player that I received in the mail kind of threw me off, for I was expecting something similar to the record player that was in our living room. We had a console stereo with four speakers built in that kicked out some nice sounding music, but what I received was more like the record players my teachers used in school, which was a little, gray box record player with one speaker connected in the front and no base at all. Nevertheless, I was still grateful to have the record player as reading was a passion of mine.

Even though I enjoyed reading, I rarely did for the fear of being talked about by my classmates and friends when I would have to put the book close to my eyes to see the words. I remember one time a classmate was walking past my desk as I was reading my textbook and he pushed the back of my head with such force that it caused me to slam my face into the book and my desk.

The record player and talking books that you received were loaned to you by the National Library Service for the Blind and Physically Handicapped (NLS), which is a national network of cooperating libraries that distribute recorded books to individuals with vision loss. The books were mailed free of charge to me in a special container that allowed me to send them back for free when I had finished listening to them

(VisionAware.org 2020). The talking books allowed me to get back to doing something that I really enjoyed: reading. This allowed me to be true to myself without the fear of being made fun of or being harassed for my visual impairment. I was able to complete book reports and assignments that required research. I would go to school and look through the card catalog in the school library to find the books that I may need to complete an assignment, and then I would request the books that I needed to help me complete the assignment from NLS. This was really a game changer for me, for it allowed me to learn and complete my assignments without having to worry about whether or not I could read the material that I needed to complete the assignment.

## TECHNOLOGY ON THE JOB

Employers have the opportunity to educate themselves about technology that has changed the game for employees who are BVI. The invention of smartphones, advances in computer technology, and apps have allowed employees who are BVI to perform their duties effectively.

Belo Miguel Cipriani, EdD, is the owner of two businesses, Oleb Books and Oleb Media. He teaches part-time at Metropolitan State University, and he is an author. In 2007, Cipriani lost his vision at age twenty-six after being assaulted by a group of men in San Francisco, CA. After undergoing numerous surgeries, he was diagnosed with retinal detachment and a traumatic brain injury.

Cipriani uses apps on his iPhone to conduct work duties such as checking and writing emails and sending and responding to text messages. "The iPhone allows me to check emails, text messages, and the use of apps keeps me connected," said Cipriani. The abundance of technology today, of which we will not be able to cover completely, has opened the door for more career options as well. "The reality is that a blind person can do any job that involves a computer, and there are a slew of adaptive tech toys that make most jobs accessible, such as a portable scanner to read printed material," says Cipriani. Hopefully this helps employers feel comfortable hiring a person who is BVI.

Assistive technology plays a major role in improving the BVI employee's work experience, but it also expands a business's pool of qualified potential applicants (Kuligowski 2019). This technology is being used to increase, maintain, or improve functional capabilities of people who are BVI (Kuligowski 2019). With that being said, assistive technology plays a major part in creating a diverse and inclusive work environment. These technologies help employees who are BVI in completing important job duties without assistance from others. Everyone in the organization benefits from an effective, accessible workspace. Productivity of all employees increases, the talent pool grows, and the organization has created the potential to acquire more customers (Kuligowski 2019). In a 2018 study conducted by Accenture, they found that companies that regularly hire people with disabilities have a higher revenue, net income was almost double, and employee retention was close to 90 percent as compared to businesses that do not (Kuligowski 2019).

Qudsiya Naqui is an Attorney and Policy Researcher diagnosed with Leber's Congenital Amaurosis. This is a condition that mainly affects the retina (MedlinePlus.gov 2020). Naqui uses a screen reading program called JAWS, or Job Access With Speech (BOIA.org 2017). This allows her to conduct internet searches, write documents, read her emails, and create presentations. Programs like JAWS reads the content from the computer screen to its readers. They also offer speech and braille capabilities to be used on majority of your computer applications (Zielinski 2019). The Bureau of Internet Accessibility says JAWS supports all Windows operating systems that have been released since Windows Vista. JAWS can also read and work with many types of HTML pages like websites and web-based applications (BOIA.org 2017). Employers can purchase this screen reading software for around a $1,000 (Zielinski 2019).

People who are BVI often have access to screen magnification software that makes the screen easier to view. Mary Lively and Brian Banks both used ZoomText Magnifier/Reader. Ms. Lively, who was diagnosed with retinis pigmentosa (RP) in 1989, used ZoomText while working in the accounting department for a collection agency, and Mr. Banks used it while attending college at The University of Akron. Zoom-Text is a fully integrated magnification and reading program tailored for low vision users. This program enlarges everything that is displayed on your computer screen. It also echoes your keystrokes while you are typing on your keyboard. ZoomText reads emails, documents, and websites (ZoomText.com 2019). The cost to purchase the magnifying software is $875 (ZoomText.com 2019).

People who are BVI can even navigate travel these days with the use of their smartphones. The smartphone allows you to make calls by either saying the number or the person's name that you would like to call. There are apps like VoiceOver that help people who are BVI move about through their day (CoolBlindTech.com 2018). VoiceOver makes it easy for people who are BVI to use their devices (CoolBlindTech.com 2018). Everything that is done on their phone is communicated verbally to the user so they can hear what they are doing. That includes making a phone call to someone, sending a text, and utilizing an app (CoolBlindTech.com 2018).

Naqui does a lot of traveling for her job, and she feels that it is much easier for her to travel with the technology that is available to her today. "There is so much technology now. Being able to call an Uber is much easier than trying to figure out how to hail a taxi," said Naqui. She books her own flights and downloads airline apps so she can have her electronic boarding pass on her phone. This will allow her to know what gates to go to for her connecting flights without having to worry about finding someone to assist her in locating the gate for her connecting flight. Naqui does not even worry about getting to the airport, getting to her gate, or how she will get to her hotel because the use of her smartphone makes her business travel a smooth process.

**THE BENEFITS OUTWEIGH THE COSTS**
Even though there is a cost for assistive technology to accommodate employees who are BVI, it is not an outrageous expense to the company. Also, employers that hire persons with disabilities can qualify for tax credits. "Employers do not realize that there are a lot of tax write offs for them in regards to purchasing technology or making the environment more

inclusive," says Cipriani, blind Founder and Digital Inclusion Strategist of Oleb Media. When it comes to purchasing assistive technology for employees that are BVI, employers can qualify for Disable Access Credit from the Internal Revenue Service (IRS) (Chaney 2020). According to business trends, this is a non-refundable annual tax credit for making a business accessible to persons with disabilities (Chaney 2020). This credit is allocated to small businesses that earn a maximum revenue of $1 million or had thirty or less full-time employees in the previous year (Chaney 2020). Businesses can apply this credit to an assortment of costs like sign language interpreters for the hearing impaired (Chaney 2020). They can purchase readers for employees that are BVI. Any adaptive or modified equipment can be purchased under this tax credit (Chaney 2020). The production of print materials in accessible formats such as braille, audio tape, and large print. Also, employers can apply this tax credit to the removal of barriers in buildings or vehicles that may prevent a business from being accessible by people with disabilities (Chaney 2020).

Employers have assistive technology available to their employees that are BVI in the products that they are already using to operate their business. "I explain to them that the technology that you've already bought is a reasonable accommodation," said Mike Hess, Executive Director and Founder of Blind Institute of Technology (BIT). Many tech companies like Apple, Google, Microsoft, and Dell offer built-in accessibility features such as voiceover, display accommodations, speech recognition, automatic subtitles, screen magnification, and keyboard customizable adjustments (Kuligowski, 2019). For example, Microsoft offers Accessibility Checker to make sure that all documents can be read by individuals with disabilities. This assistive technology looks out for missing descriptive hyperlinks, extra whitespace, improper page breaks, and any other inconsistencies that may interfere with comprehension (Kuligowski, 2019). Accessibility technology can increase productivity in business for not just employees with disabilities, but for everyone that is employed with the company. For that reason, every employee that works for the organization should know about the accessibility features in all of the equipment that they are using to perform their job duties (Kuligowski 2019).

## ACHIEVING DIVERSITY AND INCLUSION

The Americans with Disabilities Act (ADA) requires employers to provide applicants and employees with disabilities reasonable accommodation that allows them to have an equal employment opportunity. Perkins School for the Blind suggest that employers modify their employment application so that it can be easily read by computer software like JAWS and ZoomText (Perkins.org). We should provide employees who are BVI with the assistive technology they need to perform their job just as well as their sighted counter parts. Make sure that employee portals, message boards, and any other sites that the company may use are accessible to the employees who are BVI (Perkins School for the Blind 2021). Any type of computer training needs to be modified to give the employee who is BVI individualized instruction to learn the system changes properly, as the software that they may be using to accommodate their lack of vision may require specific keyboard commands in order for them to perform the new job requirements properly (Perkins School for the Blind 2021).

To ensure that they are meeting ADA guidelines for accessibility, employers can reach out to businesses that can assist them in maintaining compliance. Cipriani's business, Oleb Media, assists businesses in making sure their websites, apps, and content are within the federal and state access requirements. Cipriani said, "I founded Oleb Media because I noticed that while many organizations want to be digitally inclusive, they lack the internal resources and time to address access barriers on their websites, apps, and content." Business News Daily suggests that businesses research appropriate companies to assist them in maintaining ADA compliance when it comes to accessibility by attending Assistive Technology events so businesses can network with various vendors (Kuligowski 2019). When they meet with vendors, they need to ask to see their Web Content Accessibility Guidelines (WCAG) conformance statement (Kuligowski 2019). This statement allows clients to see that a business's digital properties are in compliance with web accessibility guidelines (EssentialAccessibility.com 2018). Employers also want to know if the vendors make the products themselves or just a retailer (Kuligowski 2019). They will want to request information from a few vendors so they can compare the products and services. Businesses need to make sure they test the products before making a purchase to ensure that it serves the purpose for which they have requested the product (Kuligowski 2019).

Employers should consider making sure that their software with accessible technology is setup properly so that the assistive technology of the employees and job seekers who are BVI can read the content that is being displayed. This helps create an inclusive, accessible work environment that benefits all employees in the business. Assistive technology can help improve productivity. The use of apps on computers and smartphones have allowed employees who are BVI to perform almost any job that they are qualified to work in. The improvements to old technology like JAWS and Zoom-Text has helped employees that are BVI be more productive in their duties. Businesses can form partnerships with companies like Oleb Media to make sure that their contact, websites, and apps are ADA compliant and accessible to the BVI community. There are a lot of assistive technologies that are available to employees for free from the products that the company is already using; moreover, employers may qualify for a tax credit for making their business accessible to disabled employees. This will create an inclusive work environment with happy, productive, and dedicated employees.

Now that we've talked about the history and the struggles of the BVI over the past one hundred years, let's explore what makes this diverse group of people so exceptional at what they do. We will talk about the principles that make the BVI so extraordinary in the workplace and what makes them such great team members.

---

**THE BOTTOM LINE**

- Assistive technology helps increase a business's talent pool, which helps create a more diverse work environment.
- Having an accessible workspace increases productivity for all employees.

- Enhance workforce desirability by including employees who are BVI, then increase revenue and employee retention within your organization.
- Businesses may qualify for a tax credit for hiring employees who are BVI. The purchase of assistive technology can be a tax write off as well for the company.
- The use of apps on computers and smartphones have allowed employees who are BVI the opportunity to pursue every job they are qualified to work. Improvements to old technologies like JAWS and ZoomText have also helped employees who are BVI be more productive in their job duties.

# PART II

# THE SKILLS OF THE VISUALLY IMPAIRED

# CHAPTER 4

# THE SCIENCE OF OUR SENSES: HOW SENSES WORK

———

Have you ever wondered how the brain works with the senses of a person who is BVI? By the end of this chapter, you will be able to identify how their senses can be an attribute to their employer's success. The everyday skills that this population uses on a daily are what employers expect of everyone employed with their organization.

## HOW THE BRAIN WORKS: A BALANCING ACT

I was at home doing some research when I came across this article about two blind brothers, Bradford and Bryan Manning, who were diagnosed with Stargardt disease (Sehwani 2019). This eye disease is an inherited disorder of the retina that usually causes loss of vision during childhood (Stargardt Disease 2021). The Manning brothers decided to go shopping together. Once they arrived at the store, they split up to go their own separate ways and decided meet back up once they were done shopping. After they were finished shopping and met back up with one another, they realized they both bought the same identical shirt (Sehwani 2019). Normally, people buy clothing on what it looks like or a particular color they are looking for. Bradford and Bryan made their purchasing decision based on touch (Sehwani 2019). A lot of people who are BVI will use their hands to shop for the softest material in a clothing item before making a purchase, and this is exactly how both brothers ended up with the same shirt (Sehwani 2019).

After reading this article, I wanted to know if this was just a coincidence that the brain really increases other senses in people who are BVI to compensate for their vision loss. If this is the case, employers can learn how the other senses of potential job candidates that are BVI will step in and fill the void of their vision loss in order to perform the job that they are asked to complete.

I remember when I was younger, I was having a conversation with my mother about my hearing. She told me that I have exceptional hearing because of my vision impairment. She told me, "You can hear a mouse piss on cotton. Your hearing is so good." I still laugh at that today, so I decided to investigate whether or not the brain enhances the other senses to replace vision loss.

## SUCCESS STORIES

In 1989, I started working for Sears and Roebuck inside Rolling Acres Mall in Akron, Ohio. I only applied for the job because my childhood friends were applying for jobs with the store.

They had a hook up with someone that worked in human resources who was going to put in a good word for them. I was already working night maintenance for a hypermarket store called Twin Valu. A hypermarket store is the combination of a grocery store and department store (Quain 2018). I told myself that I would work at Sears for the summer if I got hired, but it never crossed my mind that they would offer me a job. To my surprise, I received a call from the stock and receiving department supervisor, Linda Putnam. She wanted me to come in for an interview. After having the interview, I was offered a job in customer pickup. In this position, you carried large-ticketed items like electronics, large appliances, and carpeting to customer's cars after they made their purchases. I decided to accept the position. After working there for the summer, I quit my job with Twin Valu to remain working with Sears.

After working at Sears for about a year, my supervisor asked me to become a dock worker. I was excited to be working on the dock, for it was less stressful than taking items to customer's cars. Also, the guys that worked on the dock, Mike and Dave, were my friends. We got along very well. One day we had some down time at work, and we were sitting around talking. We ended up having a conversation about my vision. I was telling them how I have exceptional hearing. I was trying to educate them on how my other senses were enhanced to supplement for me being visually impaired. They were not buying my story, but we were close with the manager of the hearing department. Mike suggested that we go over to the hearing department so I could take a hearing test.

Once there, I explained to the manager of hearing aids about my good hearing. She informed Mike and Dave that what I was saying was true, but they still wanted proof. She setup the equipment for me to take a hearing test. She instructed me to go into the soundproof room and put the headset on. During the test, I would hear a tone in one ear, and I would raise my hand to indicate in which ear I heard it. She began sending the sound to the headset. The sound was a soft beep. I began raising my left and right hand to acknowledge which ear I heard the sound in. After completing the hearing test, my results were perfect. I heard every sound that was sent to the headset. Mike and Dave were shocked and impressed.

David Hunt, wine maker and owner of Hunt Cellars, believes that a person who loses one sense is sharper in their other senses because they depend on them more to make up for the sense they have lost (A Blind Winemaker's Philosophy for Success 2018). He attributes this to his wine success. He once took a winemaking course at The University of California at Davis. The class was instructed to pick out the different aromas in the wines they were tasting, and Hunt got them all right (Alimurumg 2013). Hunt once tasted wine from one of his competitors. After tasting the wine, he told the wine maker that the wine tasted like it was made in a concrete vat, and that turned out to be true. The competitor demanded to know how he knew. Hunt told him, "I don't know." He went on to say it was "goofy" (Alimurung 2013). Based on experiences like this with rival winemakers, Hunt has been accused of cheating. He can tell how much wine he pours into a glass by listening to the sound of the wine as the glass fills up. He said, "The pitch changes as it gets to the top." (Alimurung 2013).

Christine Ha, also known as "The Blind Cook," is a chef, writer, and TV host. Ha is also the first blind contestant to appear on the Fox hit show *Masterchef,* and she ended up being the winner of the third season in 2012. Ha is diagnosed with neuromyelitis optica (NMO). This is a central nervous system disorder that essentially affects the optic nerves in the eye and the spinal cord (Neuromyelitis Optica 2020). Since Ha does not have her sense of sight, she uses her sense of taste to really break down the ingredients in the dishes that she prepares. Since she is not distracted by a person's appearance when she comes in contact with them, she focuses more on what they are saying. Ha listens to people very carefully because she has one less sense to use to gather information. When she meets someone, Ha cannot identify ethnicity unless they are speaking with an accent. She does not know what type of clothing they are wearing, and she does not see the other person's facial expressions. All Ha has to rely on is her hearing, and the reduced distractions allows her to focus more carefully on the information that the other person is communicating.

## THE SCIENCE BEHIND THE FIVE SENSES

Research conducted by Massachusetts Eye and Ear found that the brain increases other senses in blind people. The brain makes new connections in those with early blindness, and they are not found in sighted people. These connections enhance non-visual abilities, like heighten senses, and cognitive functions such as memory and language. One of the lead doctors of the research, Dr. Merabet said, "This tells us that, in the case of blindness, the brain rewires itself so that it can be more responsive to non-visual information: things like smell, hearing, and touch. The brain rewires itself . . . to use the information at its disposal so that it can interact with the environment in a more effective manner. Even though we've already observed these compensatory behaviors, we now have a brain basis for this" (National Eye Institute 2017).

Research has shown us that the brain rewires and increases other senses of a person who is BVI to compensate for their vision loss. Now the question is how can those other senses, hearing, taste, touch, and smell, benefit employers? Our senses are not there to just provide us with the ability to taste our favorite foods or smell the wonderful flowers that you received from your significant other. They can impact our productivity (Rizzo 2014). Employers can utilize the other four senses of their staff that are BVI to influence their productivity on the job.

Some people believe that the sense of smell is one of the most important senses. "Smell is arguable the most indirectly powerful of all senses, as the olfactory bulb is part of the limbic system, or the emotional and memory center of the brain" (Bromberg 2018). Pumping in scents like lemon into the company atmosphere can increase productivity. Lemons help enhance concentration and energy levels, and pleasant, subtle scents can lift moods and decrease stress levels of all employees (Rizzo 2014). A lot of companies like hotels, restaurants, and retail stores are using scent marketing to increase their customer's spending habits (Bromberg, 2018). Employers can use these same companies to come up with the best scent for their employees to continue a productive atmosphere throughout the organization.

There is a reason you are always reminded to keep the noise down in the library. "Ambient noise, such as the inside of a coffee shop, enhances creativity compared to both low and high levels of noise" (Rizzo 2014). Moderate sound allows our imaginations to run freely. "If you can hear someone talking while you're reading or writing, your productivity can dip by up to 60 percent" (Bromberg 2018). Employers should consider purchasing sound masking technology, for it will improve employee focus by 47 percent and short-term memory accuracy around 10 percent (Bromberg 2018).

Foods and drinks you consume can have a direct link to being productive in the workplace. "A wandering mind is key to creativity. However, drinking too much caffeine can make you too focused" (Bromberg 2018). Employers that provide lunch for their staff should consider meals that have a low glycemic index like fish, brown rice, and mixed vegetables (Bromberg 2018).

The sense of touch is connected with feeling comfortable and welcomed (Bromberg 2018). When designing the interior of the workspace for employees, consider using natural materials. "It's a well-known fact that natural materials like wood and textiles are often associated with a 'warm, cozy feeling'" (Bromberg 2018). This combination helps to improve productivity (Rizzo 2014).

---

**THE BOTTOM LINE**
- Perceptive employees function better than imperceptive ones. There is a host of research that demonstrates that employees that are BVI are some of most perceptive workers in the labor force.

- Employees that are BVI are some of the most adept at identifying creative ways to use their other senses to increase their productivity in the workplace.
- Open the door to a new perspective, rely less on old technology, and discover new outlooks with a BVI representative.

# CHAPTER 5

# MASTERS OF
# THEIR SENSES

---

**CONSUMER TO CREATOR**

Based on their experience using their sense of touch shopping at the store and purchasing the same shirt, the Manning brothers decided to start a clothing company. They wanted to bring awareness and raise funds for medical research to cure eye disease, so they promised to donate all proceeds to the medical research. The Manning brothers do not take any salary from the business. They worked with experts in design and production in fabric to come up with the perfect merchandise (The Story of Two Blind Brothers - Interview with Bradford Manning and Bryan Manning 2016). All of their clothing is based on the sense of touch. This gives a sighted person the experience of how a person who is blind shops all of the time (Two Blind Brothers | Shop Blind 2021). You go into the store where you cannot see the brand, price, or color, but you can feel the item of clothing to determine if it will be something that you will be comfortable in wearing around (Is My Brother's Greatest Weakness a Secret Weapon?

| Bradford & Bryan Manning | TEDxCharlottesville 2018). Bradford Manning said, "Your greatest challenge is your greatest gift; we wouldn't be standing here without ours" (Is My Brother's Greatest Weakness a Secret Weapon? | Bradford & Bryan Manning | TEDxCharlottesville, 2018). They also wanted to help other people who are blind and visually impaired (BVI) improve their quality of life, so they decided to have all their merchandise manufactured at the Dallas LightHouse for the Blind as 70 percent of their employees are BVI (Is My Brother's Greatest Weakness a Secret Weapon? | Bradford & Bryan Manning | TEDxCharlottesville, 2018). The Manning brothers plan on running this business until there is a cure for these eye diseases. They want to be role models for other people who are BVI. They believe you should not let your challenges keep you down but you should make something positive from them.

Finding a cure for blindness has been a passion of the Manning brothers since they were both diagnosed with Stargardt disease. They wanted to create a movement to raise money for research.

Launching their business in May of 2016, they released a video on Facebook that received a lot of comments thanking them for bringing awareness to the eye disease Stargardt and appreciation for them sharing their story. They appeared on *Ellen*, who presented them with a check for $30,000 from Shutterfly to purchase $30,000 worth of t-shirts to help the Manning brothers continue funding research to find a cure for eye disease (Is My Brother's Greatest Weakness a Secret Weapon? | Bradford & Bryan Manning | TEDxCharlottesville, 2018).

## SPEAKING THE SAME LANGUAGE

Aaron Richmond is a thirty-year-old online teacher and podcaster that happens to be blind. He is diagnosed with Peters' Anomaly, which is an eye affliction that occurs in an area at the front part of the eye known as the anterior segment (US National Library of Medicine 2020). He is also diagnosed with glaucoma. This is a group of diseases that can damage the eye's optic nerve. It occurs when the fluid pressure inside the eyes slowly rises (US National Library of Medicine 2021). Richmond also has congenital heart disease.

When Richmond was conducting his job search to obtain employment, he came across an opportunity to teach English as a second language. Richmond read the job description and requirements, and he knew he was qualified for the job. He knew this was a job that he would enjoy and really wanted to help others from different parts of the world learn to speak English. Richmond was struggling with how to disclose to the potential employer that he was blind. As he was beginning to apply for the job, he realized that all he needed to submit was a short five-minute video introducing himself. It was considered a video interview. His employer reviewed the video, and they were impressed with what they saw from Richmond. They decided to hire him.

Even though he never had to disclose his blindness, his employer realized over time because Richmond told his students that he was blind. His employer has been supportive of him as an employee who is blind. He has been teaching English as a second language online for nearly six years, and he loves his job. Richmond said that he shows up every day, and he is committed to his employer. "I work almost every day of the calendar year and I have been doing that for five-and-a-half years," said Richmond. As a teacher, he uses his heightened hearing to compensate for his vision loss. "As a teacher, I have to be an active listener," says Richmond. Since he works online teaching students from all over the world, Richmond has to listen to hear if a student is struggling with speaking. Being an active listener and being able to identify when a particular student is struggling helps keep his students interested and motivated in learning the language.

## PLAY TO YOUR SENSES

According to the Houston Sinus and Allergy website, people who are BVI would make good audio engineers, editing, mixing, and creating sounds. This career will allow this population to find employment in television, music, movie, radio, and video gaming industries.

The Houston Sinus and Allergy website also posits that there are opportunities due to heightened senses of smell, such as jobs in the perfume industry. People who are BVI would make good perfumers. Perfumers are the experts on creating perfume compositions or even retail perfume managers in a department store. They would also make good aroma therapist. They use plants, flowers, and herbs in treatment and therapy.

When posting job opportunities, consider methods that focus on the particular skill that is really required of the job and alternative methods to applying will present you the chance of hiring candidates with the required skills that you are looking for in an employee that you would have not even considered during the traditional way of having applicants apply for jobs.

People who are BVI can go into the wine industry like David Hunt and become a sommelier, or wine expert. They are in charge of the wines in restaurants and retail establishments. They also pair wines with the food on restaurants menus (Sedgwick 2018). There are more career options for people with a heightened sense of taste like research chef, which is the person that creates new foods for restaurants and food manufactures. A person who is BVI can pursue a career as a food scientist. They work with engineers to come up with methods to mass produce foods while ensuring quality control (Ronca 2015).

---

**THE BOTTOM LINE**

- Leverage employees who are BVI to create twenty-first century consumer experiences by designing for all five senses.
- Improve methods to applicant screening by focusing on key skills that describe the actual needs of a job.
- Foster a culture that rewards overcoming challenges. Employees who are BVI are masters at overcoming obstacles. Gain insights into the culture of overcoming.

# CHAPTER 6

# DEDICATION

———

Although the blind and visually impaired (BVI) community has a 70 percent unemployment rate, that does not mean that they cannot be dedicated and loyal employees. This population is an untapped market for employers. They have a global workforce of thousands of workers for employers to consider hiring. A May 2002 VCU RRTC National Research Study of Employer's Experiences found that employees with disabilities are just as capable and productive when it comes to timelines, punctuality, task consistency, and work speed.

## EMPLOYER IS FAMILY

"Fifteen years ago, when I talked about hiring blind people, I was stonewalled by human-resource colleagues […]. Now it's a completely different conversation. They're sold on the idea; they just need to know how to make it work," said Charles Curtis, Human Resource Director at Radcliffe Institute for Advanced Study (Associated Press 2013). Employers that consider hiring applicants that are BVI are employing someone that is committed to the success of the organization and is planning on being a part of the organization for a long time.

In 1986, I was put on academic probation and had to sit out of The University of Akron for a year. I guess they wanted me to get a little more mature, and I definitely agreed with that, because I was not taking college seriously like I should. I was skipping class just to have lunch with my friends. I thought it was like high school: just memorize everything and show up for the test. It did not dawn on me that you had to apply the information in the book and the lecture notes to a situation. I was also in the process of looking for another job. I ended up getting hired as a busser and kitchen helper at the Georgian Room restaurant located inside O'Neil's Department Store. This was a fancy lunchtime restaurant in the heart of downtown Akron.

My main responsibility was assisting the waitresses in cleaning off the tables after the guest were finish eating, setting up and maintaining the salad bar, and helping out the kitchen staff and dishwasher as needed. Working here was like being with family. All of the kitchen staff were women, and all of them were my mother. I would go to each of them for different things and issues I would have, and it was not always work-related either. The restaurant opened at 11:30 a.m. I had to be there at 10 a.m., but I would make sure that I was there around 9:30 a.m. just in case Darren, my coworker, needed some help unloading a truck or changing the grease in a fryer.

I rarely missed any days of work in the three years I work there. I remember in 1988, my brother's high school football team had made it to the state championship game. The game was played at The Ohio State University in Columbus, Ohio. I had not missed any of his games all season, but I decided to go to work. I did not want to put the burden of my responsibilities on one of my coworkers, for they were already busy with their own work. Betty, my manager, did not know I was not going to the game until I came into work that morning. She said I could have gone. They would have managed. I told her that I did not want to put pressure on someone else to handle my job when they are already busy with their own duties. She appreciated that, and she allowed me to listen to my brother's game on the radio in the kitchen. They ended up winning the state championship as well.

During the holiday season, Betty would hire another busser to assist me because of the high volume of foot traffic we would get from holiday shoppers. In the past, some of the bussers helping us out for the holidays could not cut it, so she asked me one year if I knew of anyone that would want to work. Betty trusted me and valued my work ethic, so she was hoping that I knew of someone with similar work qualities as mine. I informed her that my friend Bobby was home from school and was looking for a job. Based on my word, she hired him, and she was really impressed with his work ethic and drive. She thanked me for referring him.

I really enjoyed working with such wonderful people, and I had planned on working there at least until I graduated from college, if not longer. In 1989, O'Neil's went out of business after my third year working there. Betty was so impressed with my work ethic and how much of a team player I was that she talked the O'Neil's management team into giving me a severance check. I was so grateful for that because I was not entitled to receive any money at all except for my last paycheck. Employees that are BVI are dedicated to their employers. They take the needed time to ensure that they arrive at work on time. Moreover, they stay after work hours to make sure that everything is ready to go the next day without any complaints.

## MY EMPLOYER GETS 100 PERCENT

"People who are blind and low vision work successfully in many fields. The problem-solving skills and can-do attitude blind and low vision people use to cope with their disability makes them tenacious employees who know how to think creatively about challenges they encounter" (National Technical Assistance Center, 2021).

Brian Banks, the retired chef who is blind, has always viewed himself as a dedicated employee. "I always knew that I was dedicated because anything I do, I commit to 100 percent, so I've never had an employer question my dedication," say Banks. His employers have questioned his ability to perform a job, but never his dedication. Banks always showed up on time and completed whatever task he had to do. He was employed as a chef at a private school in Akron, Ohio, and he took the responsibilities of his job very serious.

Banks would start out his day waking up at 6 a.m. so he could be at work by 8 a.m. He would shower and get dressed into the clothes that he laid out the night before. He had school-aged children in the home as well that attended the school where he was employed, so he had to make sure they were out of bed and ready to go when the SCAT bus arrived to pick them up.

The SCAT bus is a special service for individuals with disabilities. It is a part of the Metro Regional Transit Authority in

Akron, Ohio. The SCAT service does not give you an exact time they will pick you up. They give you a half an hour window of time when they will arrive. Banks needed to be at work at 8 a.m. The SCAT bus would be at his home between 7 and 7:30 a.m. He had to have his children and himself ready to go by seven so they could be on time.

Once he got to work, he would prepare and serve breakfast to the students who would come for breakfast. After cleaning up everything from breakfast, he would begin preparing the food items for the lunch menu for that particular day. After lunch, Banks would clean up and put everything away so he would be done around three, the time that he got off work.

Banks would do whatever he needed to do to make sure that everything ran smoothly in the school cafeteria. There had been times that he was schedule to get off work at three, but the food service delivery truck had not arrived yet. Banks would not leave until the truck arrived, and then he had put all of the food items from the delivery away. This also allowed him to know where everything was when he was ready to use it to perform his duties as a chef efficiently. If Banks did not put the food items away, there would be total confusion when they began looking for them. For this reason, he did not mind working overtime to make sure everything was in its proper place because this made his job much easier to perform.

**OUR CONTRIBUTION**
Dedicated employees have great passion for the work that they are doing. They come to work and are on time, ready to start. They are self-starters, and they get things done.

They are passionate about their work. They are respectful and courteous to staff and their customers. Also, they are adaptable when it comes to change. The applicant that is BVI possesses the same skills as the applicant who has sight. According to the Mississippi State University National Technical Assistance Center on Blindness and Low Vision, people who are BVI are dedicated workers who are less likely than other workers to leave their current employer for another job. Joe Strechay, Enthusiastic Professional Consultant, said in an article posted on the New York Daily News website, "Visually impaired people tend to be dedicated workers: less likely than others to miss a shift or quit the job, and no more likely than others to sue in the event of dismissal." They tend to have better attendance at work than sighted employees. The employee who is BVI tends to be more loyal to their employer. If you are an employer with a high turnover rate and you are looking for employees that are loyal and dedicated to their work, then give this population a chance. They are hardworking self-starters and dedicated job seekers looking for an opportunity to display their work ethic.

According to Oden, in 2002, Walgreens decided that they wanted to come up with a way to offer new job opportunities to individuals with disabilities. They came up with a foundation of systems, machines, and processes when they were constructing their new distribution center in Anderson, SC. The center was created so that it would be inclusive for employees with cognitive and physical disabilities. In order for this to happen, the distribution center was constructed with flexible workstations, elevators for those employees who cannot walk up and down stairs, touch-screen computers with large icons, and easy-to-read type for the visually impaired, and new systems to assist all employees in working efficiently.

In 2007, the distribution center opened. Walgreens partnered with local agencies that worked with the disability community so they could obtain trained people with disabilities to be employed with Walgreens in their distribution center. Other than designing their facility to be inclusive for people with disabilities, they did not have any lower expectations for their employees with disabilities. "The center offers equal pay and equal expectations of performance" (Oden, 2021).

Walgreens used training and experiential opportunities to dissipate any stereotypes that their management team may have about the capabilities of people with disabilities being employed with the company, and every employee at Walgreens participated in disability awareness training.

By employing people with disabilities at their distribution centers, Walgreens has learned that their workers with disabilities are more efficient workers and they stay employed with the company longer. The absenteeism has decreased, safety incidents are 40 percent lower, and they realized that the cost to accommodate employees with new technology and education is minimal.

Carlos Cubia, Vice President and Global Chief Diversity Officer of Walgreens Boots Alliance, Inc., which is Walgreen's parent company, said "Employees with disabilities bring so much to organizations. They help us foster collaboration and to better connect with customers. They enhance overall employee engagement, and their unique perspectives help us drive innovation [...]. Supporting and employing those with disabilities is the right thing to do, and it's good business" (Walgreens Newsroom, 2019).

---

### THE BOTTOM LINE

- When employers invest in employees who are BVI, they're investing in employees that are committed to their employer. Employees who are BVI truly have the best interest of the company at heart.
- Employees that are BVI go the extra mile to ensure that their job responsibilities are being performed effectively and efficiently.
- Employees who are BVI stay employed longer with the organization than non-disabled employees.
- Employees who are BVI have fewer accidents on the job and therefore may be cheaper to insure.

# CHAPTER 7

# ADAPTABILITY

———

The adaptable employee is not afraid of change. They do not get agitated or confused. The adaptable employee accepts change with ease and focuses on the steps that are needed to make the change work (Alcocer 2021). According to Study. com, adaptable employees experimenting is the way that they prefer to learn without worrying about failure. Adaptable employees can adjust in a moment's time, are visionaries who are proactive and prepared, and they possess a positive, professional personality.

## ADAPTABILITY IS A TAUGHT SURVIVAL SKILL

People who are BVI learn adaptability skills to survive in their day-to-day lives. They go through programs such as Texas Health and Human Services and LightHouse for the BVI to learn adaptable skills that are essential to living independently at home and in the community. They are taught how to move from one location to another safely, efficiently, and effectively. They learn adaptability skills that are transferable while participating in Daily Living Skills training courses from certified rehabilitation specialists.

After losing her sight to the point where she can only identify light, Mary Lively participated in programs offered from both agencies to learn adaptability skills to maintain her daily lifestyle. She is seventy-five years old, or "seventy-five gorgeous" as she told me during the interview. She was diagnosed with Retinitis Pigmentosa (RP) in 1989, which according to the National Eye Institute website is a group of extraordinary genetic disorders that involves the collapse and loss of cells in the retina. Lively is not totally blind. She is able to see some light but cannot identify specific objects.

Lively uses her adaptability skills very well to navigate through her day-to-day activities without skipping a beat. She has learned to live with her limitations and not depend on her sighted friends. Lively uses a red-and-white cane to identify hazards that she may trip over like cracks in the sidewalk, poles, and dropped items in her path. People who are BVI that have to use canes tend to sweep their cane from side to side to clear their path from obstacles that may be in their way.

People that possess adaptability skills are creative thinkers. Lively came up with a creative way to identify any other stumps or bumps in her path that her cane may have missed. A lot of people think she walks with a limp, but Lively actually drags her right foot as a guide because her cane does not pick up everything all the time. When she is walking and moving her cane back and forth, it may miss some items, but her dragging right foot ensure that Lively's path to her destination is clear. Some people who are BVI have to learn how to adapt to a lifestyle without sight or having low vision, but some of them have to learn to adapt to having a guide dog to assist them with their day-to-day activities as well.

In his book, *Blind: A Memoir*, Belo Miguel Cipriani tells the story of adapting to life after becoming blind due to an assault. He had to undergo numerous surgeries, and he was diagnosed with retinal detachment and a traumatic brain injury. At the age of twenty-six, he had to learn how to maintain his independent lifestyle while being blind. One aspect of his life that he had to learn to adapt to was having a guide dog, as Cipriani was never into pets. He actually felt that it was crazy how people with dogs would consider them as their children. Cipriani felt dogs required too much of his time with cleaning up dog hair and drool. This view changed one day when Cipriani was attempting to cross a busy intersection in San Francisco on a rainy day. The rain had affected his hearing, and that is one of his senses he uses to cross streets. As he stood there trying to figure out what to do next, he heard a jingling noise approaching him. It was another person who was blind with their guide dog, and the dog was wearing a harness with bells on it. They were standing next to Cipriani at the corner of the intersection. Cipriani heard the blind individual command the dog to move forward, and they went on their way across the street while he was still standing there, unsure what to do. As he stood there, frustrated trying to cross the street, a man approached the intersection and asked if he could assist Cipriani across the street. Cipriani allowed the gentleman to help him get to the other side of the street. After they made it across the street successfully, the man suggested that Cipriani should get a guide dog, and he agreed.

Cipriani attended Guide Dog for the Blind (GDB). They are a guide dog school that prepares guide dogs to serve people who are BVI. This training constantly challenged his spirit and worked his bones in ways that he never thought of. During his training, Cipriani walked with several different dogs of all sizes. What he learned was that he could get around much faster with a guide dog than he ever did walking with his cane. Cipriani felt that his life would be different with his guide dog, for he would not get lost and stab himself with his cane anymore. His guide dog was a yellow lab named Madge, and she was a handful for Cipriani. Madge was not following his commands, and this frustrated him. He never had any experience with having a dog before. Madge wanted to walk in opposite directions than where Cipriani wanted to go. Madge would disrupt the training sessions while the other guide dogs sat quietly. Cipriani did not know that having a guide dog would be so difficult. Madge would not listen to his commands. It got so bad that he thought about leaving the program.

Things started to get better when Cipriani began to think about everything that Madge had to go through to become his guide dog. She had to go through a significant change just like he did. Madge had to endure social skills training, and complete months of guide dog training. Both Cipriani and Madge had to learn to adapt to each other and the changes in their lives. After working together in their training classes for a while, Cipriani no longer had the connection with the environment that was required to move around with his cane. He learned to pick up new signals from sound and smell. He listened for the sound of people going in and out of doors to locate entrances to buildings. Cipriani used scents from restaurants and coffee shops to know his locations. Even though they were still struggling a little in their training together, Cipriani was going to make their partnership work.

Everything finally came together one day in their training. They had to go out on a rainy day to navigate through a traffic obstacle course. Cipriani was nervous about going out, as they had not done well in completing traffic obstacle courses. It was pouring, so it was hard for Cipriani to rely on his hearing. He had to put his trust into Madge guiding him along the course through the city. Once Cipriani directed Madge which way to go, she followed all his commands without any problems. Madge was alert and made sure Cipriani was moving along safe and sound. She even coursed her body in front of him when they came to a stop. This was the most connection that both of them had with each other since they met.

## THE STAR CAN SHOWCASE ADAPTABILITY

Adaptable employees can adjust to change, which makes them the foundation to the success for their employers according to Study.com. Job seekers that are BVI have been trained and execute adaptability skills in their daily lives. According to the Washington State Department of Services for the Blind, people who are BVI use adaptive techniques and skills to accommodate vision loss. Hiring professionals can level the playing field when it comes to interviewing job seekers who are BVI, and this can be done by implementing the behavioral style interview. These interview questions allow the interviewee to share how they used a particular skill in a situation and share the results of their actions (Parris 2020). The interviewee can use the STAR interview method to answer the behavioral interview questions. STAR stands for Situation, Task, Action, and Results (Parris 2020). This method allows the interviewee who is BVI to talk about a specific story that highlights how they used a particular skill in a real-life situation.

The Lane 4 Performance website identifies adaptability, which is being able to quickly acquire new skills and behaviors as it relates to change, as a soft skill. People who are BVI have to use adaptability skills as part of their everyday life to be productive citizens. During the interview, the interviewer could allow the BVI interviewee to communicate their adaptability skills from how they manage a daily lifestyle in a sighted world. According to Janet Smith, Acquisition Specialist, it does not have to be a work experience to identify if an interviewee has adaptability skills. Adaptability skills can come from someone transitioning experience from high school to college, volunteering, and learning life skills from a community organization.

Smith said, "You can assess if someone has adaptability skills by conducting a behavioral interview." You want the interviewee to communicate their specific experience in their own words on how they used adaptability skills in a particular situation.

---

### THE BOTTOM LINE

- Employees who are BVI are masters of adaptability. This is a skill that is taught to the BVI community as a matter of survival.
- Employees who are BVI are creative thinkers.
- Partner with various agencies that teach adaptability skills to the employees that are BVI to educate themselves on the various training that this population goes through to learn the skill of adaptability.

# CHAPTER 8

# RECALL

———

Having a good memory in the workplace is good for business. Employees who have a good memory learn and retain information that relates to the performance of their job, which increases productivity. Having a good memory will allow you to remember important dates, facts, and deadlines that you are required to meet (Block 2017). Companies with employees that have good memories can be leaders in their industries (Jeanetta 2017).

## MEMORY IS A MATTER OF SURVIVAL

Our brains constantly use our short-term memory, which is called working memory. Working memory involves the storage and the manipulation and process of information (Block 2017). Working memory can be viewed as being mentally online (Block 2017). In an article on Frontiers, a study was conducted that determined that people who are BVI have a higher working memory capacity than sighted people. Also, people who are BVI have to rely more on auditory input to obtain information they may need to get them through life's challenges, so they also have better memory than their sighted counter parts when it relates to auditory input (Röder, Rösler, and Neville 2001). To learn why good memory is so critical to workplace success you need to look no further than professional chef Brian Banks.

## BRIAN BANKS IMPROVISES MEMORY TO ACHIEVE SUCCESS

When Brian Banks, the fifty-six-year-old retired chef was attending The University of Akron, he registered with disability services on campus. They would assist any student with a disability with anything that would help with the success of your college experience. One of their most popular services for people who are BVI was providing a note-taker for your courses. They would pay another student that worked out of their office to come to your class and take notes for you. If they did not have a student available at the time of your class, they would allow you to ask another classmate in your class to take notes for you.

Banks had a note-taker for his lecture courses, but they did not work out too well for him because the note-takers would write his notes in handwriting instead of typing, so this prevented him from being able to read the notes. He had to rely on his memory more than the notes that he was provided from the note-takers. To overcome this challenge, Banks devised his own method of learning the material. While the professors lectured, Banks would be writing out his notes to study later, but most of the time he would take notes as a step of repetition. This process helped him memorize the material that was being lectured during the class. Preparing your memory for the workplace is not always an easy task, but there are a few tricks that will assist you in making the process a little easier.

## DR. MONA MINKARA'S DICTATION TO MEMORY

Dr. Mona Minkara uses her memory when delivering her lectures to her students at Northeastern University. She sits down with someone from her staff as she creates her lecture notes. They read the material to her, as this helps Minkara memorize the mathematical derivations for her Bioengineering course. This must be precise so that it does not confuse her students. While the person is reading the information to her, she is memorizing the information and writing down what is being said to her. Even though Minkara cannot see what she is writing, it solidifies the information in her memory.

Minkara will start out memorizing the major topics for that particular lecture. After she has the major topics memorized, she moves on to memorizing the subtopics and any other key information that needs to be discussed during the lecture. Her staff and students are always impressed that Minkara can deliver a complete lecture line by line and pages of long mathematical derivations. How does a good memory make you more detailed-oriented?

## MEMORY GIVES A COMPETITIVE EDGE

Memory is very important to Belo Miguel Cipriani's day-to-day activities. "As a blind person, what I use the most is my memory," says Cipriani. "As a person who is BVI, you have to plan your everyday activities, which may require you looking up and memorizing bus options." He has to memorize how many steps it takes to get to the intersection to avoid walking into oncoming traffic. Often when he is out with his friends, they rely on Cipriani to tell them their waiter's name, and what street were we on, or what was the zip code. He said for a person that is BVI, memory is a matter of life or death. Something could happen to them while they are out, so they need to know their location.

As a business owner, Cipriani uses his memory to compete with competitors and satisfy his customers. He feels that memory is underutilized in society today. "No one knows each other's phone numbers, no one knows emails, and they have to look up stuff or ask their smart devices," says Cipriani. This gives him the upper hand with his business. He memorizes his client's phone numbers and email addresses without having to look them up. When he has a purchasing meeting with his staff to discuss what equipment they are going to purchase for a client, Cipriani will memorize the entire purchase. He knew the equipment they were going to need, the price, and the product number. He did not have anything to write the information down at the time, so he memorized all the information needed to make the purchase. Cipriani memorizes this information because he does not want to lose things and have to go back and do it all over again.

In business, time is money. Cipriani said having a good memory in business makes you more detailed oriented. "I think I am a very attentive business owner, and that has made me an effective leader because I'm always paying attention to detail," says Cipriani. He met with a client on a sales call one day, and she had ordered some items from his company, and Cipriani memorized what she had purchased from him. The next time that he met with this client, he informed her that he remembered what she had ordered previously and went ahead and placed her order for her. The client was very pleased with his attention to detail. She said no one has ever done that for her, and even her husband is not that attentive to her. Cipriani feels that people who do not have a disability underutilize their memory. Since he does not have sight, he uses a lot more of what he has, such as his memory. This goes a long way with his business because he is more detail oriented. Also, his business will operate more effective and efficiently.

## MEMORY STATS DON'T LIE

A study conducted by the Department of Psychology at Chemnitz University of Technology in Chemnitz, Germany and Experimental and Applied Psychology at Vrije Universiteit Amsterdam, Netherlands showed that a child with a visual impairment has better working memory capacity than kids with sight. The study compared 249 children from ages of six to sixteen. The children either had vision or were visually impaired. Visually impaired included both blind and visually impaired. The study was conducted in South Africa and Austria.

The Wechsler Intelligence Scale for Children IV (WISC-IV) was used to measure the working memory capacity. The results of the test showed that the children who are BVI had a higher working memory capacity then the children with sight. This test also revealed that children who were blind had a higher working memory capacity rate than the children who were visually impaired.

A behavioral-electrophysiological investigation was developed to test the hypothesis that blind people have better auditory verbal material memory than sighted people. The test consisted of eleven blind and eleven sighted individuals to participate in the investigation. An incidental memory paradigm was administered to the participants. They listened to eighty sentences which ended with a semantically appropriate or inappropriate word. Next, the recognition phase began, and all the sentence terminal words were presented again, randomly merged with the same number of new words. The participants indicated whether or not they heard the word in the initial study phase. Event-related brain potentials (ERPs) were recorded from twenty-eight electrode positions during both the encoding and the retrieval phases. The results showed that people who are blind encode auditory verbal material more effectively than sighted people (Röder, Rösler, and Neville 2001).

There is still more research to be done, but there is growing evidence to show that people who are BVI demonstrate an enhanced capacity for memory retrieval. They have more accurate memories, can store more items and with a higher fidelity, and demonstrate greater ability across both long-term and short-term memory than their sighted counterparts.

---

**THE BOTTOM LINE**
- A good memory is an important attribute to success. Many employees who are BVI have been known to have exceptional memories. Some even practice ingenious mnemonics tactics to help commit new things to memory.

- Another successful attribute of employees who are BVI is they pay attention to detail. When it comes to sales, there can be no better closer than remembering the small details of a client or customer.

- Employees that are BVI are able to take in more information that is presented to them verbally, process the information, retain the information to memory, and then retrieve it later than their sighted coworkers.

# CHAPTER 9

# CREATIVE PROBLEM-SOLVING

———

One of the key skills that employers look for in a potential employee is problem-solving. Problem-solving helps you identify why an issue is occurring and what steps to take to resolve that dilemma (Doyle 2020). To problem solve, you must identify the issue that you are having, come up with a plan to resolve that issue, put the plan in action to fix the issue you are having, and then analyze to see if your plan worked to address the issue you were having (Doyle, 2020). Problem-solving skills may be acquired from previous work experience, but there are those individuals who also learn problem-solving skills from their day-to-day life experiences.

On the podcast The Talent Angle with Scott Engler, Anil Lewis, Executive Director of the Jernigan Institute at National Federation of the Blind said, "I'm a blind guy, and the world is not built for blind people. It's a world for the sighted, and we at the National Federation of the Blind advocate that blind individuals acquire a skill set and a problem-solving ability to deal with this world . . . in a non-visual fashion." Mr. Lewis said that this means that individuals who are blind and visually impaired (BVI) are problem solvers going through their everyday lives. People who are BVI learn and use problem-solving skills to assist them in overcoming challenges they face going through real life experiences to survive.

## PONDERING MY TRAVELS

In July of 2014, I went to Philadelphia, PA, for a business trip. My cousin and I decided that we were going to sell T-shirts commemorating Independence Day. Since Philadelphia was the first capital of The United State of America, they have a huge July Fourth celebration, so we decided to tap into that market and make some money selling T-shirts.

I purchased myself a ticket online to go to Philadelphia on July 2. I wanted to get there a few days before the holiday so I could go with my cousin to look over the merchandise before we had to make our final payment. My flight left Akron-Canton Airport around 6 a.m. with a connecting flight in Detroit, MI. I would arrive in Philadelphia around 12 or 12:30 p.m. After purchasing my ticket, I realized that I did not have anyone to take me to the airport that early. I did not want to have my parents to have to wake up that early and come by my house to pick me up and take me to the airport. Also, my cousin informed me that he would still be working at the time that I would get into Philadelphia. I have a lot of relatives in Philadelphia, but a lot of them do not have cars or driver's licenses. They ride SEPTA, which is their public transportation system. In a report from the mymove website, Philadelphia was in the top five best US cities for public transportation. According to The Balance Careers, the first part to problem-solving is identifying the issue that you need to resolve.

I began analyzing what caused this dilemma that I was in. I had never experienced this situation before where I did not have a ride to and from the airport when I have traveled to visit relatives. I was wondering how this came about, which is step one of problem-solving. I should have checked with family members that I felt would be able to get me to and from the airport before I purchased my ticket to see what their availability would have been. I tend to not think when I have a great idea on my mind that I want to accomplish.

Step two of problem-solving is generating interventions, which is brainstorming possible solutions. Now I need to figure out a way to get to and from the airport on July second. I sat around thinking about the options I had. I called Metro RTA. This is the public transportation for Akron, OH. I wanted to know if they had a bus that went to the Akron-Canton airport early enough to catch a 6 a.m. flight. The customer service representative informed me that they did not have a bus going to the airport that early. I thought about catching a cab, but I was afraid there may not be one available around the time that I needed to leave my home. I decided to call them anyway to see if they thought there would be a cab available that early. The dispatcher on the phone informed me that they could not guarantee any cabs availability at that time unless I scheduled a pickup. I did not know I could do that. I was so happy that I called instead of assuming. I scheduled a cab to pick me up around 4:30 a.m. on July 2 from my home. The next thing that I did was call my cousin so he could tell me which train I needed to catch from the airport to get to his house. He is not good at giving detailed instructions, so I also went on SEPTA's website to check the routes and prices. I was able to print out the schedules of the trains I needed to take to get to his house. I was so excited that I got my travel plans all arranged and ready to go, so I set down to go over my plans to get to the Akron-Canton Airport on time from my house and get to my cousin's house from the Philadelphia International Airport. This is the third step of problem-solving: evaluating solutions to the problem.

On July 2, I woke up at 3:45 a.m. to get ready to leave for the airport. This is the fourth step of problem-solving according to The Balance Careers: implementing a plan. I had everything packed ready to go because I packed the night before. I do not like to rush to get ready the day I plan to travel because I always forget something. I knew if I had forgotten something there would be no turning around to go get it since I was riding in a cab. Everything was going according to plan, for the cab showed up blaring its horn at 4:20 a.m. I know it woke my neighbors up.

The cab ride to the airport was about a fifteen-minute ride. There were a few people in line to check in with the ticket agents, but not a large crowd. That is why I love flying out of the Akron-Canton airport versus the Cleveland Hopkins airport. When I fly, I like to check my suitcase and carry my backpack on the plane. This allows me to move quickly through the airport just in case I may need to run so I do not miss my connecting flight. Also, it allows me to navigate through the airport to find the gate for my connecting flight.

Being visually impaired, I always have to be proactive, for anything can happen. One time I was flying, I could not see the sequence of the gate numbers and I thought my gate was at the end of one corridor, and come to find out it was at the total opposite end of the terminal. Sometimes, I have to find my gate on the screens located in the airport terminal because there may not be a ticket agent available to assist me. I am visually impaired, but people do not realize that at times when I approach them for help. My vision does not require me to have a cane or wear sunglasses to filter out light. I tend to get strange looks from people for asking for a gate number when I am standing right in front of the monitor.

I have never missed a flight because of my vision. Knock on wood! Nowadays I download the app for whatever airline I am flying, so I already know what gate to go to for my connecting flight. If the gate changes, I get an alert of the change. Modern day technology is a great asset for people who are BVI, and I love it.

I checked my suitcase with the ticket agent, and I headed over to TSA. I took my shoes off and placed them in the bin along with my other carry-on items and pushed everything down the conveyor belt along with my backpack. Today I have TSA pre-check. This allows me to go through a separate line at the TSA, and I do not have to remove any articles of clothing. It is a much quicker process, and this benefits me being visually impaired. I do not have to locate the items I took off and this gives me more time to locate my gate. I left the TSA station and walked to my gate. I boarded my plane without any problems and arrived in Detroit a little early.

I got assistance from a ticket agent in Detroit to assist me in identifying my gate number for my connecting flight. I had about two hours or so before my flight for Philadelphia departed, so I walked to the gate that my flight was leaving out of. I like to go to my gate of my connecting flight when I first arrive at the airport to make sure there are not any changes. For instance, they could reassign the flight to another gate or the flight time could change. Also, I will already know the location without having to rush and find it when it is time to board. There were no changes. I was hungry, so I decided I would grab something to eat. Whenever I get something to eat at the airport, I always eat at an establishment that is close to my gate. This allows me to hear any announcements regarding my flight and keep eye contact on the activity at my gate. I cannot identify what the people are actually doing, but I can recognize mass movement of people that are lined up to board a plane. I finished eating and went to my gate to get ready to board the plane. The flight departed on time to Philadelphia. I took a nap during this flight, for I felt calm now that I made it on my connecting flight without any issues. I slept all the way to Philadelphia.

When I arrived in Philadelphia, I got off the plane and proceeded to baggage claim to get my suitcase and headed for the train. The baggage claim signs are normally over head as you are walking down the hall, so they are easier for me to recognize. The picture of the suitcase helps as well. My mother taught me to tie something around the handle of my suitcase that stands out to help me locate my bag without a problem, so I had red yarn tied around my handle. This was very helpful, for all the bags look alike going around the conveyor belt, and the majority of the suitcases are either black or blue.

After I retrieved my bags, I headed to catch the commuter train that takes you into the Gallery Mall in Center City, which is their downtown. The train goes under the mall, and I would transfer to catch the EL. The EL is the elevated train that rides above the city except when it enters Center City. I boarded the commuter train and road it for about thirty minutes to the Gallery Mall. I love riding public transportation in any cities that I am visiting, for it gives you the pulse of the city. It makes me feel energized. When I arrived at the Gallery Mall, I hopped off the train and walked over to the EL station to get the next EL train headed to Frankford Transportation Center at the corner of Bridge and Pratt Street, which is the last stop for the train. This was wonderful for me, for my cousin lives on Pratt Street and a block from the transportation center. This ride was old hat for me, for I have been riding this train all my life.

Once I got off the EL, I walked a block to my cousin's house. He was not there, but he told me that he would leave a key under the mat. I was nervous, for my cousin can be forgetful at times. The key was there, and I was happy. This completed a very successful journey for a person who is visually impaired. I sat in my cousin's living room drinking one of his cold Heineken beers, thinking about how this journey to Philadelphia was a great success. This is the last step of problem-solving, assessing the solution's effectiveness. I would not have been able to make it to Philadelphia being a person with a vision impairment without the use of my problem-solving skills. People may read this and think that is nothing, but it is a challenge for a person who is BVI-living in a sighted world without problem-solving it first. Employers should begin to recognize that people who are BVI have to always be prepared to problem solve at the drop of a hat, for everything does not always go as planned.

## MARY LIVELY'S LINEN MUST MATCH

Since she began losing her vision, Mary Lively had to learn to problem solve. Even before she lost her vision, she has always maintained a home where everything was kept neat and in its proper place. After losing her vision, she had to problem solve solutions to continue to keep up an orderly home with everything in its right place. One of Lively's concerns was not being able to keep her colored linen sets together with their appropriate color set. She knew this would be an issue for her, so Lively sat down one day to brainstorm solutions that would allow her to keep her bedsheet sets together with their appropriate colors since she can no longer identify the different color bedsheet sets that she has.

Lively decided she would try keeping the sheets in large bags. She has one bag for each set. She went to Walmart and purchased enough two-and-a-half-gallon bags to store each of her bedsheet sets in their own separate bag. She folds the sheets and pillowcases small enough that each set fits into one bag easily. When it is time to change the linen on her bed, she will grab one of her bags and put it on her bed. She will go wash the dirty linen that she took off the bed and return the entire set to a bag. This process has been a wonderful solution for Lively to keep her linen sets together.

## OUTSIDE-THE-BOX THINKING IS AN ASSET TO BUSINESS

According to the National Center for Health Research, 78 percent of people who are BVI live in urban areas, which requires them to problem solve on a daily basis. If they decide that they have to leave their home for a particular reason, they will have to decide on how they are going to get there. Let's say they decide to ride the city bus. A person that is BVI would have to problem solve which bus route to take, so they may have to contact customer service either by calling them on the phone or using their accessibility technology to look up the information either on their phone or computer to identify the time they would have to leave to arrive at their destination at a particular time. The person who is BVI would need to make sure they have enough change for the bus fare. This may require them to actually distinguish between the different coins and paper currency they have to identify if they have the correct change or not. Moreover, they may need assistance from someone to do that. If they do not have correct change, they will need to identify somewhere close to their home and bus stop that they can get change to pay for their bus ride.

People who are BVI would be a great contribution to any employer. Their problem-solving skills are the same skills that enhance a business, for they are active listeners. They analyze a situation before jumping right into it. Individuals who are BVI think creatively to overcome the obstacles they deal with daily. Employers these are some of the most hardworking and dependable people you will ever meet.

"Talk about thinking outside the box; just the nature of people with disabilities and the lives we live requires us to think out of the box on a regular basis, which I think is a tremendous addition to any team," said Anil Lewis during an interview on the podcast show The Talent Angle with Scott Engler.

## BEHAVIORAL INTERVIEW REVEALS SKILL

Janet Smith is a Talent Acquisition Specialist and owner of TalentSmith, which is a niche recruitment agency that hires human resource professionals to fill various human resources positions for companies that are in need of Identifying top talent for their open positions. Smith has been working in the world of human resources for over twenty years. She has progressed from a human resource generalist to working in the field of recruitment and staffing. The positions that she has held over the years have varied, but most of it has been in recruitment. Smith talked about different ways employers can identify problem-solving skills in a potential candidate who may be interviewing for a position but may not have that much work experience, like a person from the BVI community. She said companies can create specific situational assessments for specific positions to see how the interviewee would solve the problem.

Smith identified another way that employers can also determine if a potential employee has good problem-solving skills. This was also mentioned in chapter seven of this book to help employers identify adaptability skills of an interviewee, which is a behavioral interview. This interview method is when employers focus on an interviewee's past experiences at work, school, and in life. For those candidates that might not meet every requirement listed in the position description and candidates with less experience, the interviewer would ask the interviewee that is BVI to give an example of a challenging situation where they had to solve a problem, and what was the outcome of that situation.

"The best way to answer behavioral interview questions is with the STAR method." said Smith. The most important thing for employers to know is that while people who are BVI may not have a lot of work experience, they problem solve on a daily basis. Smith said get the history from the interviewee so they can tell you exactly how they would handle a situation. Smith said, "Most of the time, past performance is an indicator of future behavior."

## THE OVERLOOKED PROBLEM SOLVERS

According to Career Builder, problem-solving is a universal job skill that applies to any job position in every type of business. Employers look for this skill when looking for new hires to join their company, for a good problem solver is quick to identify the issue at hand and coming up with a plan to put into action to resolve the problem. Employers have at their disposal an untapped market of people who problem solve every day.

"As a blind man that travels the world, I literally have to problem solve all of the time," says Belo Miguel Cipriani. Since people who are BVI do not have a lot of work experience to show their problem-solving skills from a situation from a current or previous job, employers can design assessments that allows the interviewee to identify how they would resolve a problem if they were employed with their company.

"A company can generate a specific test or story to see how someone would solve that problem," says Smith. Employers can focus on the BVI interviewee's challenges they had to deal with in their daily life experiences that they had to problem solve. "If it's not on the resume, it definitely can be part of the behavioral interview questions that you can ask them," says Smith. Employers can ask the interviewee to give them an example of a challenging situation that they experienced where they had to use problem-solving skills. Employers will get individuals in which problem-solving is a major part of their day-to-day life experiences. The employee who is BVI is a major asset to any employer, for they will bring an out of the box view on how resolve problems.

---

## THE BOTTOM LINE

- Problem-solving is a part of the daily activities of a person who is BVI.
- Obtain a different perspective on how to resolve a problem by employing a person who is BVI.
- A behavioral interview is a great way to identify skills from an interviewee who is BVI that may not have much previous work experience.
- Take advantage of a pool of natural problem solvers that are traditionally overlooked by competitors.

# CHAPTER 10

# MOTIVATION

---

Motivated employees make it easier for businesses to succeed. Without having motivated employees, a company puts themselves at risk of not obtaining their goals; moreover, they may be in jeopardy of going out of business (R. Heryati 2019). Motivated employees are committed to getting the job done. They help a business increase their performance by being productive workers. Applicants that are BVI are eager to work, and they are motivated to contribute to the success of a company if they are given a chance. According to the American Foundation for the Blind, in April 2017 the employment rate for BVI workers was 35 percent. They can perform the responsibilities of the job if they are given the opportunity. DuPont conducted a performance survey of 811 employees with disabilities in 1990. The results showed that 90 percent of the employees with disabilities rated average or greater in job performance compared to 95 percent of employees who did not have a disability.

## JAMIE MURPHY STEPS UP USING JAWS

People who are BVI are motivated to work. They want to be given a chance to contribute to a company's success. A motivated employee gives their best effort to every task that is asked of them. Jamie Murphy is a thirty-six-year-old Rehabilitation Counselor, and she has been working for the State of Ohio's Bureau of Vocational Rehabilitation (BVR) for nine years. She was diagnosed with an eye condition called Leber Congenital Amaurosis. According to MedlinePlus, this is an eye disorder that affects the retina. This disorder generally affects people at birth. Murphy is a great example of a motivated employee.

Murphy is not afraid of new technology. She loves discovering new gadgets, finding new product features, and learning how things work. She is especially fond of accessible technology and will seek out any new tech that can assist her in performing her work duties better. Over the years, Murphy has taught herself how to use the iPhone, voiceover technology, and the JAWS system (Job Access With Speech). Murphy has gotten so good at using JAWS system that she has even become a Subject Matter expert on the program within her agency. When there are any changes with the system, Murphy will figure out the fastest way to perform the new changes and teach others.

When BVR switched timekeeping systems, Murphy was the natural choice to call on for help. BVR asked Murphy and one other subject matter expert to help teach nine other BVI coworkers on how to use the new system. Since everyone had been working from home due to COVID, training was entirely virtual. Murphy and her SME partner taught the entire team all about using the new timekeeping system using only voiceover technology and an iPad.

## USING PSE TO ASSIST MY CUSTOMERS

In 1989, I began working for Sears and Roebuck in Akron, Ohio. I was very happy to have this job because Rolling Acres Mall was very close to my house. It was just a ten-minute bus ride to work. While I only intended to work for Sears during the summer, I ended up working there for twelve years. I started out working in customer pickup, but my last job was selling shoes in the shoe department. I have performed many duties and worked in a few different departments over the years at Sears.

I really enjoyed working in the shoe department, as I was into fashion. Once in college, I decided to change my major to clothing and textiles, I thought I wanted to be a fashion designer. This career choice did not last long after attending a sewing class and being the only male in the course. I figured being a sales associate in the shoe department would be my contribution to the fashion industry. I enjoyed the interaction with the customers and my coworkers. To better assist the customers that I served in the department, I would educate myself on the merchandise that we were selling. I was passionate about my work, and I wanted to give any customer that I served the best experience possible.

After working in the department for about a year, Sears implemented a new selling strategy called Pure Selling Environment (PSE). This new strategy allowed sales associates to handle any issues that the customers may have without having to call a manager. I really enjoyed this new policy for it allowed me to better serve my customers within the mission of Sears. I made sure that I learned the PSE process so I can implement the procedure the way in which Sears had trained us. I wanted it to be a great experience for my customers as well.

One day a customer came into the department with a pair of worn out and run-down Diehard work boots. He informed me that the soles were coming apart and he wanted to exchange them for another pair since they had a lifetime warranty on the soles. Now, a lot of customers that came into Sears felt that any of our merchandise that had the Diehard name on it was guaranteed for life. There were only two items of Sears that had a lifetime warranty on them, and that was the Diehard battery and Craftsman hand tools. I could tell that this customer would get upset and agitated if he does not get what he wanted.

He walked in very fast and aggressive. In a demanding voice, he told me what he wanted me to do instead of asking if it possible or even asking about the exchange policy. After serving the public over the years, you learn how to pick up those traits. I explained to the customer that there is not a lifetime warranty on the soles of these work boots, but there is a six-month warranty on the soles with the receipt. Of course he did not have his receipt, but I did not expect him to have one. These boots looked to be around ten years old. I told him that I could not honor the warranty without a receipt. If he could produce a receipt that showed these boots were purchased within the six-month time period, I would not have had any problem in honoring the warranty.

He was a little upset, but he understood the policy after I explained it to him. He told me that he did not know where the receipt was since he thought there was a lifetime warranty and Sears is the only store that sold this brand of boot. I understood what he was saying and his frustration. Using the PSE skills that I was trained on, I was very motivated to assist this customer so he could have a positive experience with me and Sears. I decided to allow him to purchase another pair of Diehard work boots at a discounted price. He agreed to the offer, and I reminded him to save the receipt for the six month warranty. He was pleased with me for working out something for him. He said a lot of other retailers would not have done anything for him.

## DECISION MAKERS

Employees that are BVI are motivated to work. They are motivated to work because they want to become an asset to their employer. They want to demonstrate to others that it is not a mistake in hiring them and they want to be viewed as a contributing team player just like every other employee at the company. They come to work on time and are excited to be a very productive worker for their employer. The Chicago Lighthouse conducted a survey of the retention rate of their employees that work in the Illinois Tollway Customer Care Center. They have employees who are blind, visually impaired, disabled, veterans, and non-disabled. The results of their survey showed that the employees who are blind, visually impaired, have a disability, and veterans had a retention rate of 1.7 years compared to their non-disabled and not veteran coworkers, who had a retention rate of just 0.9 years (Barrett-Poindexter 2019).

Employees that are BVI are motivated to be major contributors to the growth and success of their employer. In an article in the International Journal of Environmental Research and Public Health, a survey was conducted by The Social Psychology and Quantitative Psychology departments at The University of Barcelona. This survey looked into job motivation of employees with intellectual and physical disabilities.

There were 187 employees from Special Employment Centers (SEC's) in Spain that participated in the survey. They completed the Internal Motivation Scale, the Psychological Critical States (PCS), and the self-efficacy sub-scale of the Psychological Processes Scales (PPS) test. They followed the International Test Commission guidelines, and the tests were adapted to accommodations of each participant.

The results for employees with physical disabilities showed that their responsibility for outcomes and meaningfulness of work had a direct impact on motivation, so Based on the results of this survey, employers should consider hiring job candidates that are BVI, and promote them to decision making rolls within the company as well.

Employee that are BVI want to make sure they are trained and properly understand the duties and responsibilities that they are asked to perform.

Now that we've talked about the seven principles that make up the BVI employee, how can you as an HR manager, recruiter, or hiring manager create positive opportunities for the BVI workforce? In this next section you will learn about how to recruit job candidates that are BVI and how to make your business's culture more accessible and inclusive.

## THE BOTTOM LINE

- Employees who are BVI will ensure that your organizations goals are being met.

- Employees that are BVI are great assets to your company to ensure that your technology is accessible and capable of integrating other assistive technologies.

- When properly trained, employees who are BVI are willing and capable of being a major contributors to the success of their company or organization.

# PART 3

# HOW TO CREATE POSITIVE OPPORTUNITIES FOR THE BLIND AND VISUALLY IMPAIRED

# CHAPTER 11

# EDUCATING YOURSELF

---

How do employers educate themselves about employees that are blind and visually impaired (BVI)?

The answer is partnerships.

By partnering with agencies that support the BVI community, employers will find a multitude of tools to teach them how to recruit qualified BVI candidates, resources to help them create applications and processes that are accessible to the job seeker that is BVI, and most importantly, they will discover the countless benefits that come with hiring those within the BVI community.

Even though the employee that is BVI has a strong work ethic, is more loyal to their employer, and possesses training and education comparable to their sighted counterparts, they still are not given many employment opportunities.

They are just as capable as anyone in the workforce, but businesses do not want to give them a chance. One of the reasons for this discrepancy is that employers are just not educated on who the BVI employee is and how they work on the job.

## CHICAGO LIGHTHOUSE ORGANIZATION

Janet Smith, an Acquisition Specialist at TalentSmiths, said employers fear what they do not know. She thinks that education is the key to resolve employers' fears. The top two concerns for employers are performance and safety. They want to know what types of jobs a person who is BVI can perform. Employers need to learn about the BVI community and form partnerships with social service agencies like The Chicago Lighthouse, a leading service provider in the BVI community. Partnering with agencies like Chicago Lighthouse allows employers to benefit from using their assistive of technology support. Assistive technology specialists help employers to select the appropriate equipment and locate funding sources to help with the purchase of the equipment.

The Chicago Lighthouse Organization is a leading provider in services to the BVI community and a great place to start for anyone looking to discover the different kind of programs available out there. One of the primary services they offer to the BVI is Employment Services. They have certified rehabilitation counselors on staff that assess their clients' employment needs and goals. They conduct assessments to identify a client's computer and customer service skills. They assist in identifying careers their clients may want to pursue. They teach individuals how to build resumes, how to answer interview questions, provide coaching, and offer many other services that pertain to vision impairment and employment.

Clients can participate in a weekly job club where they listen to presentations on various topics such as job readiness, social security, public transportation, and money management.

The Chicago Lighthouse has a customer care center that gives their clients the opportunity to apply transferable skills that they have learned from their training. The center employs more than six hundred employees who have learned to work as a team, problem solve, and who are great listeners. This is a great opportunity for employers to learn more about the skills that employees who are BVI can bring to their company.

The Chicago Lighthouse also provides paid in-house opportunities to its clients. This gives employers a risk-free introduction to working with employees who are BVI. Employers can use Chicago Lighthouse interns to see how well their new hires perform at the jobs they need filled, and if they succeed, they can prepare for more long-term employment transition after a certain period of time.

Chicago Lighthouse provides job placement and retention to their clients. Employment counselors work with clients on creating an individualized plan for employment and obtaining a quality job. Clients may find employment with an outside employer or get hired by Lighthouse. After being employed for the first ninety days, a staff members will meet with the clients to discuss how things are going on the job and assist them in resolving any issues they may have. This is a wonderful opportunity for employers to partner with an agency like Chicago Lighthouse, for they are presenting them with trained qualified employees that will diversify their business and possess the skills needed to be successful. Employers that partner with agencies like Chicago Lighthouse will benefit from having an employment counselor to assist them in the development of individualized strategies for their employees who are BVI to strengthen their productivity and obtaining any employment goals that are set for them. Employment counselors are available to employers to assist in assessing workplace accommodations to make sure that the employees that are BVI have the appropriate equipment needed to perform their job. The counselors are available to educate employers on the best strategies on developing a workplace that is inclusive to people who are BVI. Another leading service provider in the BVI community is the Blind Institute of Technology (BIT).

## THE BLIND INSTITUTE OF TECHNOLOGY

The Blind Institute of Technology (BIT) is a small nonprofit organization in the Denver Colorado area working to enhance the professional opportunities for their clients with disabilities. Their founder and CEO Mike Hess, who is blind, informed me during our interview that BIT's business model performs as a nonprofit staffing agency for their BVI candidates.

"Our business model is completely unique in the blindness community, because we don't get paid until we get our candidates a job," says Mike Hess. They communicate to C-suites in the corporate world that professionals with disabilities have the skills that employers in corporate America have ignored. "We don't job hop, we don't get jobs and quit, and a really high percentage of us are going to get our bachelor's, master's, and double bachelor's degrees. So, it's not a lack of acumen; it's not a lack of skills. It's a lack of opportunity, and that is what BIT is addressing," says Hess. BIT's main goal is always employment for their candidates that are BVI. They look forward to the day when all of corporate America has equipped themselves to employ people with disabilities so they can have the same employment advantages as nondisabled employees.

BIT connects candidates with disabilities with Fortune 500 companies. Their main focus is placing their candidates in employment positions within the tech industry, for this is one of the top industries with a supply and demand rate of four to one in the US economy. They also assist their candidates in other high demand skill areas such as project management, data science, business analysis, and finance.

BIT also assists any employers that reach out to them in filling an open position with a qualified skilled candidate. After identifying what is required to perform the job from the employer, the staff at BIT begins their search of qualified candidates that are capable of performing the job responsibilities. They also take into account that many employers may not be familiar with the ADA guidelines when it comes to interviewing, hiring, and bringing on a new employee with a disability into their organization, so BIT gives advice to employers on what assistive technology that the new employee who is BVI may need. They help with integrating new employees with disabilities into the company. The BIT staff also provides follow-up services once their candidates are placed to make sure they are performing their job duties as expected by their employer. Companies can also register to participate in BIT's Art of

Blinders Seminar and learn the power of active listening and the benefits it brings to the company.

## SPONSOR COMMUNITY EVENTS

Employers can participate in and sponsor some events that are affiliated with the BVI community to learn how they are able to perform the same duties as sighted people. During Workplace Eye Wellness Month in March, employers could hold a company-wide event promoting the importance of wearing proper eye protection on the job. The month of May is Healthy Vision Month, so employers promote the importance of eye as it relates to overall health by hosting an eye health fair at work.

Form a partnership with your local blind organization and sponsor a White Cane Day event in your community. The purpose of White Cane Day is to educate sighted people on how the BVI community can live and work independently while being contributing citizens in their community. Also, this event showcases the accomplishments and contributions of BVI people in a sighted world. Employers could host an employment fair for people with disabilities during the month of October, which is National Disability Employment Awareness Month. This was created to raise awareness of the affect people with disabilities when it comes to employment, and it recognizes all the contributions from American workers with disabilities.

## THERE IS HOPE

We are getting better, but we are not there yet. In a study that was commissioned by the National Industries for the Blind (NIB) in 2018, the recruiting, training, and retaining of employees with disabilities has increased since 2012 by 12 percent. The survey also revealed that more hiring managers believe there are more jobs with their companies that employees who are BVI can actually perform with success. In addition, the survey showed that employers with less than a thousand employees benefited from educational programs that assisted managers and employees in learning how to work side by side with their coworkers that may have a disability has increased by 20 percent since 2012.

---

## THE BOTTOM LINE

- By forming partnerships with social service agencies and staffing agencies that cater to people who are BVI, you will learn all about the many skill that employees who are BVI possess.
- Collaborate with agencies that provide employability skills training to job seekers that are BVI. This is a great way to acquire qualified and trained employees to fill open positions you may have.
- Social service agencies offer training on the proper way to go about accommodating new hires.
- Get involved in community events within the BVI community. Show that your business is truly invested in supporting and learning all that this population is capable of.

CHAPTER 12

# HOW TO LEVERAGE STATE RESOURCES

———

According to an article posted on Accenture's website, there are 15.1 million working age individuals who have a disability residing in the United States. If businesses decide to welcome disability inclusion into their workplace, they will acquire more than 10.7 million potential applicants.

This would be an opportunity for employers to hire applicants that they have not previously solicited to work for their organization in the past who are ready and eager to work. Since there is a worker shortage due the pandemic, this is a great time to consider applicants that are BVI to fill these open positions to ensure that the company keeps performing successfully.

**PARTNERSHIPS FOR PLACEMENT**

Employers can increase their talent pool and get trained on laws that require specific accommodations when hiring a person who is BVI by forming partnerships with community-based organizations that work with the BVI community.

"By having a partnership or agreement specifically with a blind center in your community, you're targeting more people from diverse backgrounds," said Janet Smith. She went on to say employers need to be intentional and strategic with their efforts in forming partnerships with organizations that specifically caters to the BVI. These community-based organizations and employers could form a partnership where they provide trained candidates to fill open positions. Employers can form partnerships with community-based organization that serves the BVI community to manufacture their products or deliver their services. One of the best assets for any organization looking to partner with is the state's services for the BVI.

**THE STATE AND BUSINESS**

In the state of Ohio, we have the Bureau of Services for the Visually Impaired (BSVI). According to the Opportunities for Ohioans with Disabilities (OOD) website, BSVI is a part of OOD. They provide training, technology, and employability skills that are needed by people who are BVI to obtain and maintain employment. They assist their clients in maintaining an independent lifestyle by teaching their clients life skills they need to live on their own and locating gainful employment.

OOD purchases personal and work adjustment training for their clients to assist them in reaching their career goals by learning personal habits, attitudes, and skills needed to be a valuable employee. They get their clients training on proper work habits to have and an introduction into the world of work. OOD also have their clients trained on the techniques on how to compensate for the loss of sight.

Whenever needed, OOD can also help their clients get registered for vocational training as it relates to the career that the client is trying to pursue. The vocational training may be completed at a vocational school, college or university, technical school, business school, and it could be on the job training or supported training in a particular career field. They can also assist with the purchases of the supplies needed to complete the training such as textbooks, tools, and licenses. OOD will also assist businesses in purchasing the necessary equipment a client needs to start a job.

OOD can assist their clients with physical and mental restoration to either correct or modify an impairment so they can perform the job duties that are required of them by their employer. The restoration services they provide are hospitalization and surgery, artificial limbs and braces, eyeglasses and hearing aids, and occupational and physical therapy.

Once their clients have completed their specific training, OOD provides job placement assistance. Their clients learn how to prepare a resume and they conduct mock interviews to prepare their clients for the tough questions that may be asked during the interview process.

## WHAT BSVI DID FOR ME

In 1980, I was in the eighth grade at Simon Perkins Junior High School in Akron, Ohio when my counselor, Ms. Cerone, arranged for me and my family to meet a case manager, John Buchman, from Visual Services for the Visually Impaired (VSVI). Since then, they have changed their name to the Bureau of Services for the Visually Impaired (BSVI). They assist eligible individuals starting at age fourteen with low vision and blindness. BSVI offers direct, personalized services that assist their clients in acquiring and maintaining gainful employment. They also assist their clients in obtaining independence skills, so they can have the ability to live independently and productively in society. While I was in school, they arranged for me to get visual aids, large print textbooks, and talking books. They also got me a tape recorder and record player so I could listen to my talking books. They also got me a computer and computer desk towards the end of my college career.

During the summer of my junior year of high school, my case manager enrolled me in a program in Columbus, Ohio that would assist me in identifying which jobs would be best for me with my vision impairment. I went to Columbus to a rehabilitation vocational center for people with disabilities for a week. While I was there, I underwent all types of mobility, aptitude, and psychological testing to identify my skills and to determine which jobs would best fit my skill set and vision impairment.

During my first semester of college, which was the fall of 1985, I was not doing so well in school. I scheduled an Earth Science course at noon, which was when a lot of students took their lunch, so I would skip the class to have lunch with my friends. I was failing classes and not putting enough effort into studying. Also, I was feeling depressed. I didn't want to go to my family members for help, for I knew they would tell my parents that I was not doing well in school.

I decided to schedule an appointment with John to see if he would assist me in finding some employment. At this point, I had been working with John since I was thirteen years old. We hadn't always had a good working relationship. There had been times when I felt he could have done more to assist me with my vision impairment so I could be successful in whatever I was trying to accomplish. Sometimes, I would ask for equipment or visual aids, and he would give me the run around. I had been a client with BSVI long enough to know when they had the financial resources to purchase items. I would never expect anything during the last quarter of the year, for I knew their budget would be low.

When I met with John, he told me that he would have to check and make sure there was some money available in their budget to assist me in obtaining employment since it was toward the end of the year. A few weeks passed before he called to let me know he could help. He gave my name and contact information to a job coach that would reach out to me to schedule an appointment.

The job coach reached out to me, and we scheduled a time to meet. The coach informed me that we would start out buy conducting a thorough job search. His idea of thorough job search was looking in the classified section of our local Sunday newspaper, The Akron Beacon Journal, to see what jobs I was interested in and qualified for. I was also told to highlight the jobs in the paper that I wanted to apply for and then cut them out and paste them on a separate piece of paper and bring them to our next meeting. I felt like he was just giving me busy work to show John so he could get paid from BSVI. I did not want to ruffle any feathers, so I went along with the program. I wanted and needed a job to fall back on in case I got kicked out of school. Also, most employers were not giving employment opportunities to people with disabilities, for the Americans with Disabilities Act did not pass as law until July 26, 1990.

After working with the job coach for a few weeks, he came across a job that he felt would be a good employment opportunity for me. It was a telemarketing job. I would be selling light bulbs for a company that hired people with disabilities. Telemarketing jobs are great employment opportunities for people who are visually impaired, for most of the work is done over the phone. Also, you read from a script that can be memorized and the font of the script can be enlarged. I really was not excited about selling items over the phone, for I thought about how I felt when telemarketers called our house trying to sell us something. I hated them! I did understand that this was my first job, and it would give me some work experience that I could use down the road. Also, I did not want to continue being a part of the 70 percent unemployment rate of individuals who are BVI, so I took the job.

## STATE REHABILITATION AGENCIES
## UNDERSTAND BUSINESS

State rehabilitation agencies like BSVI understand that businesses are in business to make money, so forming partnerships with these state agencies can give employers a large number of trained diverse workers at their disposal. These state agencies offer internship opportunities, so employers may want to participate in a state agency internship program before actually hiring a person who is BVI. In a report by the Associated Press, Richard Curtis was Vice President of State Street Corporation, which is a financial services company in Boston. He extended an opportunity for two gentleman that were BVI to come on board for the summer. Curtis and State Street wanted to educate themselves on what accommodations they would need and what would be the challenges for any employee that is BVI. The interns' job duties were to conduct research and assist with creating company reports using Excel and other data-retrieval systems. Curtis learned that those two interns performed equally in their speed and accuracy to any of his sighted employees.

State rehabilitation agencies can help employers create a diverse work environment by providing disability training. They can assist employers in hiring trained qualified workers who are BVI. They provide follow up service to employers, for their goal is to keep their clients employed. Also, these state agencies can educate employers about workplace accessibility and the ADA guidelines

State rehabilitation agencies could reduce or eliminate a business's recruiting and training expenses, since they would be relying on the state agency to feed them trained, qualified employees. Since employees who are BVI are more loyal to their employers than sighted employees, this partnership will cut down on employer turnover cost to hire a new employee. These agencies provide on the job training to make sure that an employer and client are a good fit. Employers that form partnerships with state agencies to hire their BVI clients may qualify for a federal tax credit for employing people with disabilities. This partnership can help employers create a diverse work environment that looks like the community that they provide their products and services for. The Division of Vocational Rehabilitation Florida Department of Education says employing people with disabilities helps employers generate revenue by entering the market of people with disabilities. They will be able to create brand trust and loyalty with this population, and there could be an opportunity to create new products and services that caters to this population. Also state agencies can educate employers about workplace accessibility and the ADA guidelines.

---

### HOW TO CONNECT WITH YOUR STATE

At the end of this book inside the appendix, you will find a list of each state and US Territory's services for the BVI and/ or state rehabilitation service agency. If there is not a service listed for your state, please contact thee state rehabilitation service agency, as your service provider may be combined into one agency.

To take advantage of your states services:
1. **Identify** your states services for the BVI or rehabilitation service agency in your state by using the appendix at the back of this book.
2. **Contact** your state's agency and inform them that you are interested in hiring a BVI candidate.

3. **Create an action plan** that outlines your organization's specific needs and expectations for this partnership. Before your meeting with the representative, take time to identify your needs.

4. **Schedule** an in-person meeting to talk with a local representative to learn about all the services that they offer. Explore the different ways that your organization can benefit by forming a partnership with the state agency. At the end of the call, set up an in-person meeting with the agency rep.

5. **Engage.** Be transparent on what your intentions are for forming this partnership and be clear on what you would like to accomplish from working with their local state services.

# CHAPTER 13

# CREATING ACCESSIBLE APPLICATIONS AND INTERVIEWS

Before starting his businesses, Belo Miguel Cipriani, EdD, was a tech recruiter placing some of the world's most talented engineers at some of the world's largest companies like Google, Apple, eBay, and Hitachi. "What I liked most about recruiting was seeing the big smiles on my clients' faces when they landed their dream job," he said.

When Cipriani was looking for recruiting jobs for himself, he came across various positions that he knew that he was qualified for but was excluded from applying for these positions because he could not submit an application. "If I cannot apply for a job on the web with my accessibility software, I am being discriminated against because it's not accessible to me. . . . If the job posting doesn't allow me to submit my resume with my technology, that's ableism. That's not being really inclusive."

## ACCESSIBLE SOFTWARE IS A MUST

It is important for employers to use all of their resources to identify the right candidate for the position that they are trying to fill, and that includes people who are blind and visually impaired (BVI).

When accommodating and considering applicants who are BVI, employers must have their career website and online employment applications accessible for them to use and complete if they choose.

The applicant that is BVI does not have to disclose their disability to the potential employer. If the employer knows that the applicant does have a disability, they can ask the applicant how they would like to go about completing the hiring process. This allows businesses that are hiring to expand their employee base and target an underutilized market like the potential applicant that is BVI.

Part of the problem that employers are having is that they are purchasing software technology from their vendors that is not capable of interacting with assistive technology. Cipriani said, "A lot of employers want to buy these resume databases or all these different quizzes online and all these different tools to expedite recruiting, and they don't realize that a lot of these tools are not accessible." There was a job that Cipriani knew that he was qualified to do, which was a Human Resource Professional role with experience in working with ADA accommodations. When he went to submit his resume for the position, they required applicants to take a short quiz, and the quiz was not accessible for him to take. The quiz was gamification with scenarios with an image and things going on in the picture. Then the applicant is asked to identify what is wrong in this scenario, and this is not accessible to someone who is BVI. The irony of it all is that this company wanted to hire someone with experience in ADA accommodations.

## IS YOUR APPLICATION ACCESSIBLE?

Employers that ask job seekers to fill out job applications that know that the person is BVI should ask the individual which application process works best for them. The employer should never assume that all applicants that are BVI will complete the same type of application. They all are individuals with different types of eye conditions, and they will prefer completing the application in the format that is most comfortable to them. Employers should offer mailing or emailing the application or allowing the individuals to stop into the business to pick up an application, for they may have someone that will assist them in completing the application.

"The tools that businesses are using and buying are not designed to be digitally inclusive," says Cipriani.

If the applicant that is BVI wants to complete the form online, Partnership on Employment and Accessible Technology (PEAT) suggests the employer make sure that the application can be read by a screen reader. A screen reader is technology that assists people who are BVI in translating the information that is written on a website into speech or braille. They need to make sure that their online employment application and website have navigation elements like headers, titles, and lists for the screen reader to work properly.

Employers that use images on their employment websites should make sure they have descriptive text that can be read by a screen reader to describe the message that the image is conveying to its readers.

The applicant that is BVI using adaptive technology to complete the employment application without using a mouse will need to be able to go through and complete the form by using the tab key. Avoid using moving images on the website such as animation, slideshows, videos, and pop-ups. A lot of people who are BVI may require extra time to complete an employment application online, so employers should offer the user the option of turning off or extending the time on these types of pages. Avoid having downloads, for they have to be accessed by assistive technology as well, so consider putting all available information for the reader on the company website.

**EMPATHETIC INTERVIEW PROCESS**

The interview is one of the most important parts of the hiring process for a company. This gives the employer the opportunity to identify the best candidate for the position that they are hiring for based on the skills that the interviewee possesses to perform the required job duties. This process of interviewing someone for a job should be conducted the same for persons who are BVI as it would be for a person with sight. The person conducting the interview of a person that is BVI must be empathetic to the limitations of the interviewee's eye condition.

When preparing for the interview, the US Department of Labor suggests that the interviewer needs to make sure that they are not preparing to ask any questions related to the interviewee's blindness or vision impairment. They need to make sure that the location for the interview is accessible for a person who is BVI. Also, the interview should take place in a lighted area so that the BVI interviewee's visual acuity does not change. If the interviewer is aware that the interviewee is BVI before the interview begins, they can provide the appropriate accommodations so that the interviewee can participate in the interview process. The interviewee that is BVI may need some assistance completing some forms that are part of the company's interview procedure. The company should provide proper assistance for the interviewee to complete the forms. Also, the interviewer should inform the BVI interviewee ahead of time if there will be a test or assessment they will have to complete during the interview, for this will allow the interviewee to have enough time to request the appropriate accommodations to complete the task that is being asked of them to do.

During the interview, the interviewer should greet the BVI interviewee with a handshake. In the Planes, Trains and Canes YouTube video, "Three Ways Not to Interview a Blind Person," Dr. Mona Minkara exaggerates about shaking hands, for there is a perception that people have that people who are BVI cannot shake hands. Please do not hesitate to shake hands with the interviewee who is BVI. Once the interviewee extends their hand out to shake hands, the interviewer needs to shake their hand. If the interviewee does not offer their hand to shake, the interviewer can offer theirs and ask if can they shake their hand. The interviewer should identify themselves and any other people that may be with them. If the interviewer needs to touch the interviewee that is BVI for any reason, they need to make sure that they ask for permission first.

The interviewer will need to assist the interviewee to their seat. After asking to assist them, place the BVI interviewee's hand on the back or arm of their chair they will be sitting in and make sure that you are giving verbal instructions when giving directions. Since the interviewee is unable to pick up body language cues, the interviewer should communicate to the interviewee who is BVI when the interview is over and if they have to move to another location of the building to continue the interview. Keep the focus of the interview on qualifications and skills that the interviewee has to perform the job and not on the fact that they are BVI. Interview them the same way you would interview a person with sight.

The interviewer should make sure that they are only asking the interviewee who is BVI questions that relates to the performance of the positions that the applicant is interviewing for. If the person that is conducting the interview focuses on the interviewee's knowledge, skills, abilities, experience, and interests in performing the job that they are interviewing for, the interview will go very well for both the interviewer and interviewee who is BVI.

---

**THE BOTTOM LINE**
- To create an inclusive job opening ensure your online applications are designed to be accessible for job seekers who are BVI.

- Make sure the location of the interview is also accessible to interviewees who are BVI.
- During the interview, focus on the skills that the interviewee who is BVI is interviewing for. Remember that problem-solving, forward planning, and a willingness to experiment are all skills that are important for innovation.

# CHAPTER 14

# EMPOWERING DIVERSITY AND INCLUSION

---

## DEFINING DIVERSITY AND INCLUSION

A business's mission, strategies, and best practices that pursue diversity and inclusion are a competitive edge over their competition. In recent years research has shown that a diverse and inclusive workforce allows companies to become more adaptable, creative, and they start attracting highly skilled performers that want to be a part of their organization's success.

Diversity in the workplace is being compassionate, welcoming, and appreciating the people from different backgrounds that compose the staff of the organization. When you prioritize inclusion metrics in the workplace, collaboration is more common, group participation improves, and company culture becomes more resilient against downturns.

## TRENDS TOWARD A MORE DIVERSE AND INCLUSIVE WORKFORCE

The Boston Consulting Group surveyed employees from more than 1,700 companies in eight countries and found that 75 percent of the respondents said that diversity is increasing with their employer.

Businesses today are focused on diversity and inclusion in the workplace. It has become a popular topic recently because employers know that a diverse work environment creates stronger employee interaction, greater productivity, and enhances the likelihood of somewhere in the labor pool having the problem-solving skills necessary to get the job done.

It's wonderful that employers are beginning to understand the value of diversity and inclusion when it comes to their employees. Unfortunately, in many cases, the BVI community is not being included in this new trend of diversity and inclusion. In a report from the Return on Disability group, 90 percent of the companies said that diversity is a priority, but only 4 percent included disabilities in their campaigns.

As you know by now, the employee who is BVI can make a valuable asset to any company by increasing the talent base, enhancing company diversity, and offering unique perspectives to the decision-making processes of a company. How do employers implement a diversity and inclusion program?

## WHERE TO FIND MORE INFORMATION ON YOUR NEXT DIVERSITY AND INCLUSION PROGRAM

Service agency like Chicago Lighthouse can educate businesses about the different skills that the job seeker who is BVI are able to perform. The Blind Institute of Technology (BIT) caters to the job seekers who is BVI and offers businesses qualified and trained employees that can fill open positions they may have.

Find your State Department of Rehabilitation Services to learn more. These organizations provide training, technology, and employability skills that are needed by people who are BVI to obtain and maintain employment. They assist their clients in maintaining an independent lifestyle by teaching their clients life skills that they need to live on their own and locating gainful employment.

## HOW TO IMPLEMENT YOUR PROGRAM

Establish a partnership with your local state rehabilitation agency. State organizations that serve the BVI community can give businesses the tools they need in obtaining qualified employees. My state department is called Opportunities for Ohioans with Disabilities (OOD). They support programs like Bureau of Services for the Visually Impaired (BSVI). They provide training, technology, and employability skills that are needed by people who are BVI to obtain and maintain employment. They assist their clients in maintaining an independent lifestyle by teaching their clients life skills they need to live on their own and locate gainful employment.

Private companies like Chicago Lighthouse offer great resources for employers looking to implement Diversity and Inclusion Programs into their organization. Some of the resources that they have available includes the Chicago Lighthouse Internship Program.

Other organizations like Blind institute of Technology Recruitment Services are for those looking to hire job candidates that are BVI.

## PICTURE OF THE WORKFORCE FOR THE FUTURE

Employers need to be inclusive with their communication methods on the job. Make sure accessible communication devices are being used and available to all that may need or want to use them. When giving presentation or trainings, makes sure all visual materials being used are being described verbally for the employees who are BVI. Create a culture with all employees when entering and leaving a large gathering of employees like a meeting that everyone acknowledge that they are entering or leaving the room. Employers can take the initiative and ask their employees who are BVI how the company can assist them in performing their job effectively. People who are BVI are use to these types of conversations, so employers should not feel uncomfortable in asking. Actually, it may make the employees who are BVI feel good that their employer is reaching out first without them having to ask them.

A company's diversity equity and inclusion program looks at all aspects of the business from the start to the finish. "Whatever your business does, you're asking the question, how are we serving people with disabilities in this part of the business? Whether it's marketing, HR, or recruiting, everyone knows the products and services," says Meg O'Connell, CEO and Founder of Global Disability Inclusion. Let's look at the employment lifecycle, which is an HR term from the time an employee gets hired to the time they leave the company. The first time that a business comes into contact with an employee is during the recruiting process, and is it fully accessible for employees who are BVI. O'Connell shared a statistic from an article she read on Forbes website that only 8 percent of the companies that were polled were confident that their recruitment processes were disability-inclusive.

The next step is new employee onboarding. According to the Society for Human Resource Management (SHRM), this is the process of integrating a new employee with a company and its culture, as well as getting a new hire the tools and information needed to become a productive team member. This is the first day on the job for a new employee who is BVI, so there is a lot of paperwork that needs to be completed. The employer provides the options of having someone available to assist the employee in completing the paperwork, mail the paperwork in advance, or the employer can provide an accessible PDF. Moreover, these options should be determined by which one the employee is most comfortable with.

A company with a good diversity, equity, and inclusion program actively markets their accessibility features for people who are BVI. Their customer service team knows how to operate the features to assist customers when any problems arise. Also, every employee needs to be educated on what accessibility technology the organization offers for employees and customers. O'Connell said, "You know I say all the time that accessibility and inclusion is everyone's business." Do not make diversity, equity, and inclusion an afterthought.

# ACKNOWLEDGEMENTS

---

Life can be rough for a person who is born visually impaired without the love, support, and encouragement from family and friends who truly believe in you. These are the people that care about your wellbeing so much that they want to discourage you from pursuing activities that they feel you are not capable of doing or that may put you in harm's way, but they still support you in putting forth your best effort when you still want to give it a try.

This was my mother, Edith Kidd-Broaddus, and father, Welby C. Broaddus, Sr. They supported me through everything that I wanted to try even though I knew they were hesitant in allowing me to participate in some of those activities. I can honestly tell you today that without that type of support from my parents, you would not be reading this book right now. Mom and Dad! Let me stop, for I do not call them that. Mommy and Daddy, I really, truly appreciate you guys for being my parents, for I know it was hard at times for you guys to see me try things and fail. It was hard for me, but I am so thankful that you allowed me to go through it and fail. I do not know if you guys realize it, but that failure and embarrassment gave me character and a better understanding of who I am today. I love you guys, and I am very appreciative of the support you gave me as I wrote this book. I love you both from the bottom of my heart.

Thank you to all my interviewees. I appreciate you taking the time from your busy schedules to share your stories and knowledgeable information. Without you guys, this book would not be a great resource for HR professionals and business leaders.

Thank you to the Creator Institute and New Degree Press. Eric Koester and Brian Bies, I really am appreciative of you guys giving me the opportunity of making a long-time dream of mine of writing and publishing a book come true. The staff has been very supportive and helpful throughout the entire process, and I am grateful for that.

Thank you to my beta readers. I really appreciate you taking time out of your busy schedules to assist me in making sure that the content of the book is on point in delivering the message that I want to portray.

Thank you to Dr. Angela E. Dash for remembering that I always wanted to write a book. You shared the link for the Creator Institute and encouraged me to apply even when I was reluctant to follow through. You assisted me in staying focused and motivated to continue during the times I wanted to quit. Once my pre-sale campaign started, you were my biggest cheerleader. You purchased two copies of my book and encouraged your family and friends to purchase a copy of my book as well. I was grateful for that, but you did not stop there. When you found out that I was short on reaching my goal to raise enough funds to create an audiobook for my readers who are BVI, you took it upon yourself to make a donation without me knowing to help the audiobook become a reality. I am so glad that you believe in me and support me. I really appreciate and I love you.

Thank you to Stacey Hodoh. We became friends in kindergarten, attended the same schools together, and graduated together. Go Griffs! You have been a wonderful person and good friend of mine all those years. I want to really thank you for your wonderful generosity and support of me. Your contribution really made my dream come true of raising enough money to create an audiobook for people who are BVI that may want to purchase the book. The staff at the publishing company, New Degree Press, had to create an entire new perk just for you. Stacey I am so overwhelmed with your generosity, and thank you again.

Lastly, a *huge* thank you to all of you who purchased a book and made a donation to my pre-sale campaign so that I could raise enough funds to turn my dream of writing a book into a reality. I really appreciate the love from all of you, for I never thought I would have gotten this much support. I want you to know that the love I received from all of you throughout this process is what inspired me to keep pushing forward on those hard days that I did not want to continue, so thank you for that. I love all of you.

|                      |                   |
|----------------------|-------------------|
| Melani Walker        | David Broaddus    |
| Eric Koester         | Tara Broaddus     |
| Edith L. Broaddus    | Angela Dash       |

Anthony Broaddus

Karen Broaddus

Vickie Dent

Robert Parnell Jr.

Shalisha Holyfield

Vanessa Thomas

Tia Hall

RiAnn Davis

Sarah Broaddus

Debra Rhine

Demond Dobson

Juniper Sage

Gretchen Kainz

David Martin

Chad Winfrey

Chelsea Winfrey

Sara Martin-Stalls

Linda Woodson

Rochelle Poling

Christopher Rivero

LaWanna Holt

Monica Gooden

David T. Harris

Stacey Hodoh

Sonya Williams

Samantha Broaddus

Kathy Ann Davis

Yvette Mitchell

LaDonna Johnson

Jamaine Howard Kidd

Siddiq Washington

Treschelle Costa

Darlene Pearson

Dolly Davis

Ericka McClam

Denise McGuckin

Glenn Daniels

Eufrancia G. Lash

Katie Herman

Kathy Hullum

Mack Stephens

Marva Broaddus

Welby Broaddus, Sr.

Melody Carr

Elizabeth Tyson

Stacy Davis

Dora Evans-Lewis

Yolanda Ray

Peggy Darrell

Salima Dunn

Montoyia Weir

Ismail Al-Amin

Commission Cigar Collective

Pat Millhoff

Vence Albert Williams

Melissa Stallings

Claire White

Carl Anderson

Annie Skapin

Traci McNairy

Yvette Webster

Erica Sebree

Phyllis Lofton

David K. Horner

James Stocks
Michael Flinn
Lisa Eagle
Debra Wright
Kelli Crawford-Smith
Jerusha Palmer
Mona E. Martin
Belinda Whiteside
Harriet A. Woods
Madeleine Olson

Tracy Jones
Wendy Campbell
Zaire Lofton
Cheryl Hopkins
Antwyone Samples
Toni Stylz
Rolanda Findlay
Hugh M. H. Dash
Dion Jackson
Bryson Love

# REFERENCES

---

## NETWORKS

Job Accommodation Network (JAN) www.AskJAN.org.

Equal Employment Opportunity Commission (EEOC) www.eeoc.gov.

US Department of Justice (DOJ) ADA Homepage. www.ada.gov.

Americans with Disabilities Act National Network. www.adata.org.

---

## PRIVATE PARTNERS

These are private agencies that you can partner with to assist you in on-boarding employees who are blind and visually impaired.

### BROADDUS BUSINESS SOLUTIONS (BBS)
Phone: (234) 303-1506
Email: broaddusbizsol@gmail.com
Website: https://www.broaddusbizsol.com/

### BLIND INSTITUTE OF TECHNOLOGY (BIT)
Website: https://blindinstituteoftechnology.org/

### GLOBAL DISABILITY INCLUSION, LLC
Phone: (844) 434-4255
Website: https://www.globaldisabilityinclusion.com/

### OLEB MEDIA
Phone: (612) 568-1013
Email: info@olebmedia.com
Website: https://www.olebmedia.com/

### RISHA GRANT, LLC
Phone: (918) 581-8900
Email: contact@rishagrant.com
Website: https://rishagrant.com/

### TALENTSMITHS
Email: info@talentsmiths.net
Website: https://talentsmiths.net/

## STATE PARTNERS
This is a list of each state and US territory's vocational rehabilitation service agency and their services for the blind and visually impaired agency. The states that do not have a service agency for the blind and visually impaired listed means you must contact their vocational rehabilitation services agency for assistance.

**ALABAMA**

Alabama Department of Rehabilitation Services

Phone: (334) 293-7500

Toll-Free: (800) 441-7607

Toll-Free Restrictions: AL residents

Fax: (334) 293-7383

Website: http://www.rehab.alabama.gov/

**ALASKA**

Division of Vocational Rehabilitation

Phone: (907) 465-2814

Toll-Free: (800) 478-2815

Fax: (907) 465-2856

Website: http://labor.alaska.gov/dvr/home.htm

**ARIZONA**

Rehabilitation Services Administration

Toll-Free: (800) 563-1221

TTY: (602) 340-7771 (Maricopa County)

TTY: (855) 475-8194 (outside Maricopa County)

Website: https://www.azdes.gov/RSA/

**ARKANSAS**

Rehabilitation Services Division

Phone: (501) 296-1600

Arkansas Department of Human Services

Division of Services for the Blind

Phone: (501) 682-5463

TTY: (501) 682-0093

Fax: (501) 682-0366

Website: http://ace.arkansas.gov/arRehabServices/Pages/default.aspx

## CALIFORNIA
California Department of Rehabilitation
Phone: (916) 324-1313
TTY: (916) 558-5807
Website: https://www.dor.ca.gov/

## COLORADO
Division of Vocational Rehabilitation
Phone: (303) 866-4150,
Toll-Free: (866) 870-4595
Fax: (303) 866-4905, (303) 866-4908
TTY: (303) 866-4150
Website: https://dvr.colorado.gov/

## CONNECTICUT
Department of Aging and Disability Services
Phone: (860) 424-5055
Fax: (860) 424-4850
TTY: (860) 247-0775
Website: http://www.ct.gov/besb/site/default.asp

## DELAWARE
Division of Vocational Rehabilitation (New Castle County)
Phone: (302) 761-8275
TTY: (302) 761-8275
Website: https://dvr.delawareworks.com/

## DISTRICT OF COLUMBIA
Department on Disability Services (District of Columbia)
Phone: (202) 730-1700
Fax: (202) 730-1843
TTY: (202) 730-1516
Website: http://dds.dc.gov/

**FLORIDA**

Division of Vocational Rehabilitation

Phone: (850) 245-3399

Toll-Free: (800) 451-4327

TTY: (850) 245-3399

Fax: (850) 245-3316

Website: http://www.rehabworks.org/

Division of Vocational Rehabilitation

Division of Blind Services

Phone: (850) 245-0300

Toll-Free: (800) 342-1828

Fax: (850) 245-0363

Website: http://dbs.myflorida.com

**GEORGIA**

Georgia Vocational Rehabilitation Agency

Phone: (844) 367-4872

Website: https://gvra.georgia.gov/

**HAWAII**

Division of Vocational Rehabilitation

Phone: (808) 586-5275

Fax: (808) 586-9755

TTY: (808) 586-5288

Website: https://humanservices.hawaii.gov/vr/hoopono/about/

**IDAHO**

Division of Vocational Rehabilitation

Phone: (208) 334-3390

Toll-Free: (844) 324-3988

Website: http://www.vr.idaho.gov/

Vocational Rehabilitation Agency
State Commission for the Blind and Visually Impaired
Phone: (208) 334-3220
Toll-Free: (800) 542-8688
Fax: (208) 334-2963
Website: https://icbvi.idaho.gov/

## ILLINOIS
Division of Rehabilitation Services
Toll-Free: (800) 843-6154
TTY: (866) 324-5553
Website: http://www.dhs.state.il.us/page.aspx?item=29736

## INDIANA
Division of Disability and Rehabilitative Services
Toll-Free: (800) 545-7763
Fax: (317) 232-1240
Website: http://www.in.gov/fssa/2328.htm

## IOWA
Vocational Rehabilitation Services
Phone: (515) 281-4211
Toll-Free: (800) 532-1486
Fax: (515) 281-7645
Website: http://www.ivrs.iowa.gov/

Vocational Rehabilitation Agency
Iowa Department for the Blind
Phone: (515) 281-1333
Toll-Free: (800) 362-2587
Toll-Free Restrictions: IA residents only
Fax: (515) 281-1263
Website: https://blind.iowa.gov/

**KANSAS**

Department of Social and Rehabilitation Services

Phone: (785) 368-7143

Toll-Free: (866) 213-9079

Fax: (785) 368-7467

TTY: (785) 368-7478

Website: http://www.ovr.ky.go

**KENTUCKY**

Kentucky Office of Vocational Rehabilitation

Phone: (502) 564-4440

Toll-Free: (800) 372-7172

Website: https://kcc.ky.gov/Vocational-Rehabilitation

**LOUISIANA**

Rehabilitation Services State Office

Phone: (225) 219-2943

Toll-Free: (800) 737-2958

Website: http://www.laworks.net/WorkforceDev/LRS/LRS_Main.asp

**MAINE**

Bureau of Rehabilitation Services

Phone: (207) 623-6799

Fax: (207) 287-5292

Website: http://www.maine.gov/rehab/index.shtml

**MARYLAND**

Division of Rehabilitation Services

Phone: (410) 554-9442

Toll-Free: (888) 554-0334

TTY: (410) 554-9411

V.P. 443-798-2840

Website: http://www.dors.state.md.us/

**MASSACHUSETTS**

Massachusetts Rehabilitation Commission

Phone: (617) 204-3600

Voice/TTY: (800) 245-6543

Fax: (617) 727-1354

Website: https://www.mass.gov/orgs/massachusetts-rehabilitation-commission

Vocational Rehabilitation Agency

State Commission for the Blind

Phone: (617) 626-7509

Website: https://www.mass.gov/vocational-rehabilitation-vr-for-the-blind

**MICHIGAN**

Bureau of Services for Blind Persons

Phone: (517) 241-1100

Toll-Free: (800) 292-4200

Fax: (517) 335-5140

TTY: (888) 864-1212

Website: http://www.michigan.gov/lara/0,4601,7-154-61256_28313—,00.html

Rehabilitation Services

Phone: (517) 241-5324

Fax: (517) 335-7277

Toll-Free: (800) 605-6722

Website: https://www.michigan.gov/leo/0,5863,7-336-94422_97702---,00.html

**MINNESOTA**
State Services for the Blind
Phone: (651) 539-2300
Toll-Free: (800) 652-9000
Website: http://www.mnssb.org/
Vocational Rehabilitation Services
Phone: (651) 259-7114
Website: http://www.deed.state.mn.us/rehab/

**MISSISSIPPI**
Office of Vocational Rehabilitation
Toll-Free: (800) 443-1000
Website: http://www.mdrs.ms.gov/Pages/default.aspx

**MISSOURI**
Division of Vocational Rehabilitation
Phone: (573) 751-3251
Toll-Free: (877) 222-8963
Fax: (573) 751-1441
TTY: (573) 751-0881
Website: http://dese.mo.gov/vr/

Rehabilitation Services for the Blind
Toll-Free: 1-800-592-6004
Website: http://dss.mo.gov/fsd/rsb/index.htm

**MONTANA**
Montana Vocational Rehabilitation
Phone: (406) 444-2590
Toll-Free: (877) 296-1197
Fax: (406) 444-3632
TTY: (406) 444-2590
Website: http://www.dphhs.mt.gov/detd/vocrehab/

**NEBRASKA**

Nebraska Commission for the Blind and Visually Impaired
Phone: (402) 471-2891
Toll-Free: (877) 809-2419
Fax: (402) 471-3009
Website: http://www.ncbvi.ne.gov/

Vocational Rehabilitation
Phone: (402) 471-3644
Toll-Free: (877) 637-3422
Fax: (402) 471-0788
Website: http://vr.nebraska.gov/

**NEVADA**

Rehabilitation Division (Northern Nevada)
Phone: (775) 687-6860
Website: https://detr.nv.gov/Page/Rehabilitation_Division

Rehabilitation Division (Southern Nevada)
Phone: (702) 486-5230
Website: https://detr.nv.gov/Page/Rehabilitation_Division

**NEW HAMPSHIRE**

Vocational Rehabilitation
Phone: (603) 271-2327
Fax: (603) 271-7095
Website: https://www.education.nh.gov/who-we-are/deputy-
commissioner/bureau-of-vocational-rehabilitation

**NEW JERSEY**

Commission for the Blind and the Visually Impaired

Phone: (973) 648-3333

Toll-Free: (877) 685-8878

Website: http://www.state.nj.us/humanservices/cbvi/home/

**NEW MEXICO**

Division of Vocational Rehabilitation

Phone: (505) 954-8500

Toll-Free: (800) 224-7005

Website: http://www.dvr.state.nm.us/

**NEW YORK**

State Commission for the Blind

Toll-Free: (866) 871-3000

TTY: (866) 871-6000

Website: http://www.ocfs.state.ny.us/main/cbvh/

Adult Career and Continuing Education Services – Vocational
Rehabilitation (ACCES-VR)

Toll-Free: (800) 222-5627

Website: http://www.acces.nysed.gov/vr

**NORTH CAROLINA**

Division of Vocational and Rehabilitation Services

Toll-Free: (800) 689-9090

Fax: (919) 855-3500

TTY: 919-855-3579

VP: (919) 324-1500

Website: http://dvr.dhhs.state.nc.us/

**NORTH DAKOTA**

Division of Vocational Rehabilitation

Phone: (701) 328-8950

Toll-Free: (800) 755-2745

Fax: (701) 328-1884

Website: http://www.nd.gov/dhs/dvr/index.html

**OHIO**

Bureau of Vocational Rehabilitation

Toll-Free: (800) 282-4536

Website: http://ood.ohio.gov/

**OKLAHOMA**

Oklahoma Department of Rehabilitation Services

Phone: (405) 951-3400

Toll-Free: (800) 845-8476

Website: http://www.okrehab.org/

**OREGON**

Office of Vocational Rehabilitation Services

Phone: (503) 945-5880

Toll-Free: (877) 277-0513

Website: http://www.oregon.gov/DHS/vr/

**PENNSYLVANIA**

Office of Vocational Rehabilitation

Phone: (717) 787-5244

Toll-Free: (800) 442-6351

TTY: (717) 787-4013 or (877) 497-6545

Website: http://www.dli.pa.gov/Individuals/Disability-Services/
ovr/Pages/OVR-Office-Directory.aspx

Blindness and Visual Services
Phone: (717) 787-7500
Toll-Free: (866) 375-8264
TTY: (717) 787-1733
TTY: (888) 575-9420
Website: http://www.dli.pa.gov/Individuals/Disability-Services/

**RHODE ISLAND**
Vocational and Rehabilitation Agency
Phone: (401) 421-7005
TTY: (401) 421-7016
Website: http://www.ors.ri.gov/VR.html

**SOUTH CAROLINA**
South Carolina Vocational Rehabilitation Department
Phone: (803) 896-6500 (Columbia area)
Toll-Free: (800) 832-7526
TTY: (803) 896-6553
Website: http://www.scvrd.net/

**SOUTH DAKOTA**
Division of Rehabilitation Services
Phone: (605) 773-3195
Fax: (605) 773-5483
Website: http://dhs.sd.gov/drs/

**TENNESSEE**
Vocational Rehabilitation Services
Phone: (615) 313-4891
Fax: (615) 524-3093
TTY: (615) 313-5695
TTY: (800) 270-1349
Website: https://www.tn.gov/humanservices/ds/vocational-rehabilitation.html

**TEXAS**

Department of Assistive and Rehabilitative Services

Phone: (254) 770-5800

TTY: (866) 581-9328

Division for the Blind

Phone: (254) 753-1552

Website: https://www.twc.texas.gov/

**UTAH**

Utah Workforce Services Rehabilitation Services for the Blind
and Visually Impaired

Phone: (801) 323-4343

Toll-Free: (800) 284-1823

Fax: (801) 323-4596

TTY: (801) 538-7530

Website: https://jobs.utah.gov/usor

**VERMONT**

Vocational Rehabilitation

Voice/TTY: (802) 241-1455

Toll-Free: (866) 879-6757

Website: http://vocrehab.vermont.gov/

**VIRGINIA**

Department of Rehabilitation Services

Phone: (804) 662-7000

Toll-Free: (800) 552-5019

Fax: (804) 662-9532

Website: https://www.vadars.org/#gsc.tab=0

**WASHINGTON**

Division of Vocational Rehabilitation

Toll-Free: (800) 637-5627

Website: http://www.dshs.wa.gov/dvr/

Department of Services for the Blind (DSB)

Phone: (800) 552-7103

Website: http://www.dsb.wa.gov/

**WEST VIRGINIA**

Division of Rehabilitation Services

Phone: (304) 356-2060

Toll-Free: (800) 642-8207

Website: http://www.wvdrs.org/

**WISCONSIN**

Division of Vocational Rehabilitation

Phone: (608) 261-0050

Toll-Free: (800) 442-3477

Website: http://dwd.wisconsin.gov/dvr

**WYOMING**

Division of Vocational Rehabilitation

Phone: (307) 777-8650

Website: http://www.wyomingworkforce.org/

**TERRITORIES**

**AMERICAN SAMOA**

Division of Vocational Rehabilitation

Phone: (684) 699-1372

Phone: (684) 699-4234

Website: https://rsa.ed.gov/grantee/as/american-samoa-office-vocational-rehabilitation

**COMMONWEALTH OF THE NORTHERN MARIANA ISLANDS**
CNMI Office of Vocational Rehabilitation
Phone: (670) 322-6537
Fax: (670) 322-6548
Website: http://www.ovrgov.net

**GUAM**
Division of Vocational Rehabilitation
Phone: (671) 475-4647
Website: https://www.autismspeaks.org/provider/division-vocational-rehabilitation-dvr-1

**PUERTO RICO**
Vocational Rehabilitation Administration
Phone: (787) 729-0160
Website: https://askjan.org/organizations/Puerto-Rico-Vocational-Rehabilitation-Administraci percentC3 percentB-3n-de-Rehabilitaci percentC3 percentB3n-Vocacional.cfm

**VIRGIN ISLANDS**
Division of Disabilities and Rehabilitation Services
Phone: (340) 774-0930
Website: http://www.dhs.gov.vi/disabilities/index.html

# APPENDIX

––––––

**INTRODUCTION:**

Alimurung, Gendy. "David Hunt and the Secrets of Blind Winemaking." *LA Weekly,* June 28, 2013.
https://www.laweekly.com/david-hunt-and-the-secrets-of-
blind-winemaking/.

Blanck, Peter. "Employment of Persons with Disabilities: Past,
Present and Future." American Psychological Association.
American Psychological Association, 2008.
https://www.apa.org/pi/disability/resources/publications/
newsletter/2008/08/employment.

Kuligowski, Kiely. "How Hiring People with Disabilities Helps
Business." business.com, December 30, 2020.
https://www.business.com/articles/hire-disabled-people/.

Myers, Cynthia. "High Rate of Unemployment for the Blind."
CHROM, November 9, 2016.
https://work.chron.com/high-rate-unemployment-
blind-14312.html.

The OrCam (Blog). "Jobs for Blind People, History and Opportunities Thanks to Technology." September 10, 2019. https://www.orcam.com/en/blog/jobs-for-blind-people-history-and-opportunities-thanks-to-technology/.

Virginia Commonwealth University. "The Realities of Hiring People with Disabilities Fact Sheet." VCU RRTC. Accessed May 23, 2021. https://vcurrtc.org/resources/viewContent.cfm/589.

## CHAPTER 1: HISTORY OF DISCRIMINATION AGAINST THE BLIND AND VISUALLY IMPAIRED

American Macular Degeneration Foundation. "What Is Macular Degeneration? - AMDF." December 20, 2017. https://www.macular.org/what-macular-degeneration.

Anti-Defamation League. "A Brief History of the Disability Rights Movement." ADL Fighting Hate For Good. Accessed May 10, 2021. https://www.adl.org/media/6891/download.

Blanck, Peter. "Employment of Persons with Disabilities: Past, Present and Future." American Psychological Association. American Psychological Association, 2008. https://www.apa.org/pi/disability/resources/publications/newsletter/2008/08/employment.

Kansas Council on Developmental Disabilities. "The Disability Rights Movement." Accessed September 7, 2021. https://kcdd.org/the-council/103-general-content/249-the-disability-rights-movement.

Leon, J. "Ed Roberts." Encyclopedia Britannica, March 10, 2021. https://www.britannica.com/biography/Ed-Roberts.

Meldon, Perri. "Disability History: The Disability Rights Movement (US National Park Service)." National Parks Service. US Department of the Interior, 2019. https://www.nps.gov/articles/disabilityhistoryrightsmovement.htm.

Tiner, Joe. "Disability Legislation History." Colorado State University Student Disability Center, January 30, 2018. https://disabilitycenter.colostate.edu/disability-awareness/disability-history/.

US Department of Justice Civil Rights Division Disability Rights Section. "The Americans with Disabilities Act and Other Federal Laws Protecting the Rights of Voters with Disabilities." ADA, September 2014. https://www.ada.gov/ada_voting/ada_voting_ta.htm.

US National Library of Medicine. "Cone-Rod Dystrophy: MedlinePlus Genetics." MedlinePlus. August 18, 2020. https://medlineplus.gov/genetics/condition/cone-rod-dystrophy/#:~:text=Cone%2Drod%20dystrophy%20is%20a,the%20back%20of%20the%20eye.

## CHAPTER 2: A PERSISTENT ISSUE: THREE CASES OF MODERN DISCRIMINATION

ADA National Network. "What Is Considered an 'Undue Hardship' for a Reasonable Accommodation?" May 13, 2021. https://adata.org/faq/what-considered-undue-hardship-reasonable-accommodation.

American Foundation for the Blind. "Reviewing the Disability Employment Research on People Who Are Blind or Visually Impaired: Key Takeaways." Accessed May 2020. https://www.afb.org/research-and-initiatives/employment/reviewing-disability-employment-research-people-blind-visually.

Disability Rights Advocates. "Herrera v. New York State." September 28, 2020. https://dralegal.org/case/herrera-v-new-york-state/.

Kelley, Jeremy P. "New Law Expands Private School Voucher Program in Ohio: How It Will Work." Journal News, November 27, 2020. https://www.journal-news.com/news/new-law-expands-private-school-voucher-program-in-ohio-how-it-will-work/PQY7UWZQSZFD3D2O45S2KTUDOM/?outputType=amp.

Mayo Clinic. "Retinal Detachment." Mayo Foundation for Medical Education and Research, August 28, 2020. https://www.mayoclinic.org/diseases-conditions/retinal-detachment/symptoms-causes/syc-20351344#:~:-text=Retinal%20detachment%20describes%20an%20emergency,and%20ofloaters%20in%20your%20vision.&text=Retinal%20detachment%20describes%20an%20emergency,and%20ofloaters%20in%20your%20vision.

Myers, Cynthia. "High Rate of Unemployment for the Blind." CHROM. November 9, 2016. https://work.chron.com/high-rate-unemployment-blind-14312.html.

US Department of Justice Civil Rights Division Disability Rights Section. "A Guide to Disability Rights Laws." ADA, February 2020. https://www.ada.gov/cguide.htm.

US Equal Employment Opportunity Commission. "Overview." Accessed May 14, 2021. https://www.eeoc.gov/overview.

## CHAPTER 3: WHY NOW: THE POWER OF TECHNOLOGY

Britannica, T. Editors of Encyclopedia. "Phonograph." Encyclopedia Britannica, July 24, 2019. https://www.britannica.com/technology/phonograph.

Bureau of Internet Accessibility. "How Does JAWS Help Navigate and Read Webpages?" June 22, 2017. https://www.boia.org/blog/how-does-jaws-help-navigate-and-read-web-pages#:~:text=JAWS%20allows%20users%20to%20read,through%20a%20refreshable%20braille%20display.&text=The%20JAWS%20application%20supports%20Windows,%2C%20and%20web%2Dbased%20applications.

Chaney, Paul. "Small Business Tax Credits for Hiring Disabled Workers." Small Business Trends, February 4, 2020. https://smallbiztrends.com/2016/06/small-business-tax-credits-hiring-disabled-workers.html.

Cool Blind Tech. "How to Use a Phone If You Are Blind or Visually Impaired." February 19, 2018. https://coolblindtech.com/how-to-use-a-phone-if-you-are-blind-or-visually-impaired/#:~:text=A%20smartphone%20allows%20the%20blind,you%20would%20like%20to%20reach.

Essential Accessibility. "6 Requirements for a Web Accessibility Conformance Statement." September 28, 2018. https://www.essentialaccessibility.com/blog/web-accessibility-conformance-statement.

Kuligowski, Kiely. "What Small Businesses Need to Know About Assistive Technology." Business News Daily, July 2, 2019. https://www.businessnewsdaily.com/15185-assistive-tech-for-smbs.html.

MedlinePlus. "Leber Congenital Amaurosis: MedlinePlus Genetics." US National Library of Medicine, August 18, 2020. https://medlineplus.gov/genetics/condition/leber-congenital-amaurosis/#:~:text=Leber%20congenital%20amaurosis%20is%20an,visual%20impairment%20beginning%20in%20infancy.

Perkins School for the Blind. "Workplace Accommodations." Accessed May 19, 2021. https://www.perkins.org/services/workplace/employers/workplace-accommodations.

VisionAware. "Audio Players and Talking Books." APH Connect Center, August 27, 2020. https://visionaware.org/everyday-living/essential-skills/reading-writing-and-vision-loss/audio-players-and-talking-books/.

Zielinski, Dave. "New Assistive Technologies Aid Employees with Disabilities." SHRM. August 16, 2019. https://www.shrm.org/resourcesandtools/hr-topics/technology/pages/new-assistive-technologies-aid-employees-with-disabilities.aspx.

ZoomText. "ZoomText Magnifier/Reader." Freedom Scientific, January 2, 2019. https://www.zoomtext.com/products/zoomtext-magnifierreader/.

## CHAPTER 4: THE SCIENCE OF OUR SENSES: HOW OUR SENSES WORK

Alimurung, Gendy. "David Hunt and the Secrets of Blind Winemaking." LA Weekly, June 28, 2013. https://www.laweekly.com/david-hunt-and-the-secrets-of-blind-winemaking/.

Bromberg, Joyce. "How the 5 Senses Help Inspire Workplace Productivity." Convene. October 22, 2018. https://convene.com/catalyst/engage-5-senses-inspire-workplace-productivity/.

FoxBusinessNetwork. "A Blind Winemaker's Philosophy for Success." YouTube, September 11, 2018. YouTube video, 4:26. https://www.youtube.com/watch?v=oQvdYM8IXrU.

Mayo Clinic. "Neuromyelitis Optica." Mayo Foundation for Medical Education and Research, December 10, 2020. https://www.mayoclinic.org/diseases-conditions/neuromyelitis-optica/symptoms-causes/syc-20375652#:~:text=Neuromyelitis%20optica%20(NMO)%20is%20a,spectrum%20disorder%20or%20Devic's%20disease.

National Eye Institute. "Brain 'Rewires' Itself to Enhance Other Senses in Blind People." US Department of Health and Human Services, May 10, 2017. https://www.nei.nih.gov/about/news-and-events/news/brain-rewires-itself-enhance-other-senses-blind-people#:~:text=The%20brains%20of%20those%20who,by%20NEI%2D-funded%20researchers%20at.

National Eye Institute. "Stargardt Disease." US Department of Health and Human Services. Accessed May 21, 2021. https://www.nei.nih.gov/learn-about-eye-health/eye-conditions-and-diseases/stargardt-disease.

Quain, Sampson. "The Difference between GROCERY, SUPERMARKET, & Hypermarket Merchandisers." Chron.com, November 26, 2018. https://smallbusiness.chron.com/difference-between-grocery-supermarket-hypermarket-merchandisers-75675.html.

Rizzo, Paula. "Use Your Five Senses to Get More Done." List Producer. May 06, 2014. https://listproducer.com/2014/05/engage-five-senses-increase-productivity/.

Sehwani, Joseph. "Blind Entrepreneurs: Loss of Sight but Not Your Vision." Starfire Dynamics, March 26, 2019. https://starfiredynamics.com/blind-entrepreneurs-loss-of-sight-but-not-your-vision/.

## CHAPTER 5: MASTERS OF THEIR SENSES

National Eye Institute. "Brain 'Rewires' Itself to Enhance Other Senses in Blind People." US Department of Health and Human Services. May 10, 2017.
https://www.nei.nih.gov/about/news-and-events/news/brain-rewires-itself-enhance-other-senses-blind-people#:~:text=The%20brains%20of%20those%20who,by%20NEI%2D-funded%20researchers%20at.

Nguyen, CT. "Careers for Good Ears: 5 Interesting Jobs for People with Brilliant Hearing." Houston Sinus & Allergy, July 25, 2014.
https://houstonsinusallergy.com/5-Interesting-Jobs-For-People-With-Brilliant-Hearing.

Nguyen, CT. "Top 7 Well Paid Jobs You Can Only Get If You Have a Very Good Nose." Houston Sinus & Allergy, June 9, 2014.
https://houstonsinusallergy.com/top-7-well-paid-jobs-you-can-only-get-if-you-have-a-very-good-nose/.

Ronca, Debra. "10 Careers Where You Can Eat for a Living." HowStuffWorks, June 22, 2015.
https://money.howstuffworks.com/10-careers-eat-for-living.htm.

SEDGWICK, HANA-LEE. "What Is a Sommelier?" WineCountry.com, August 28, 2018.
https://www.winecountry.com/blog/what-is-a-sommelier/.

TEDxTalks. "Is My Brother's Greatest Weakness a Secret Weapon? | Bradford & Bryan Manning | TEDxCharlottesville." February 14, 2018. YouTube video, 17:21 https://www.youtube.com/watch?v=xZW1DoYkgiA.

The Chicago Lighthouse. "Top 5 Benefits of Hiring People with Disabilities." October 6, 2016. https://chicagolighthouse.org/sandys-view/top-5-benefits-hiring-people-disabilities/.

Two Blind Brothers. "The Story of Two Blind Brothers - Interview with Bradford Manning and Bryan Manning." May 17, 2016. YouTube video, 2:14. https://www.youtube.com/watch?v=u7mf2FcylPU.

Two Blind Brothers. "Two Blind Brothers | Shop Blind," May 17, 2021. YouTube video, 0:59. https://www.youtube.com/watch?v=Zhu-xEUb19k&t=58s.

US National Library of Medicine. "Glaucoma | Blindness." MedlinePlus, May 5, 2021. https://medlineplus.gov/glaucoma.html.

US National Library of Medicine. "Peters Anomaly: MedlinePlus Genetics." MedlinePlus, August 18, 2020. https://medlineplus.gov/genetics/condition/peters-anomaly/.

## CHAPTER 6: DEDICATION

Associated Press. "Many Employers Still Reluctant to Hire Blind Workers." nydailynews.com, November 4, 2013. https://www.nydailynews.com/life-style/health/employers-reluctant-hire-blind-workers-article-1.1506358.

National Technical Assistance Center. "Why Hire Workers Who Are Blind or Have Low Vision?" Mississippi State University, March 4, 2021. https://www.ntac.blind.msstate.edu/businesses/why-hire-workers.

ODEN. "Walgreens Case Study - May 2017." Accessed May 26, 2021. https://odenetwork.com/resource/walgreens-case-study-may-2017.

Virginia Commonwealth University. "The Realities of Hiring People with Disabilities Fact Sheet." VCU RRTC. Accessed May 23, 2021. https://vcurrtc.org/resources/viewContent.cfm/589.

Walgreens Newsroom. "Walgreens Earns Best Place to Work in 2019 Disability Equality Index." Walgreens, July 18, 2019. https://news.walgreens.com/press-center/news/walgreens-earns-best-place-to-work-in-2019-disability-equality-index.htm.

## CHAPTER 7: ADAPTABILITY

Alcocer, Yuanxin Yang. "Adaptable Employees: Characteristic & Importance." Study.com | Take Online Courses. Earn College Credit. Research Schools, Degrees & Careers. Accessed May 29, 2021. https://study.com/academy/lesson/adaptable-employees-characteristics-importance.html.

Lane 4 Performance. "The Importance of Adaptability Skills in the Workplace." Accessed May 29, 2021. https://www.lane4performance.com/insight/blog/the-importance-of-adaptability-skills-in-the-workplace/#:~:text=Adaptability%20is%20a%20soft%20skill,in%20response%20to%20changing%20circumstances.&text=Someone%20demonstrating%20adaptability%20in%20the,don't%20go%20as%20planned.

National Eye Institute. "Retinitis Pigmentosa." US Department of Health and Human Services. Accessed May 29, 2021. https://www.nei.nih.gov/learn-about-eye-health/eye-conditions-and-diseases/retinitis-pigmentosa.

Parris, Jennifer. "How to Use the STAR Method to Shine Bright in Your Interview." FlexJobs Job Search Tips and Blog. FlexJobs.com, December 14, 2020. https://www.flexjobs.com/blog/post/sar-method-answering-job-interview-questions-v2/.

Washington State Department of Services for the Blind. "Adaptive Skills / Skills of Blindness." DSB. Accessed May 29, 2021. https://dsb.wa.gov/adaptive-skills-skills-blindness.

## CHAPTER 8: RECALL

Block, Cena. "A Good Memory Is Good For Business." Sane Spaces, April 14, 2017. https://sanespaces.com/2017/04/good-memory-business/.

Jeanetta, Tony. "7 Benefits That Boost Employee Memory Improvement: TOG." The Olson Group, July 18, 2017. https://theolsongroup.com/7-benefits-that-boost-memory-improvement/.

Mayo Foundation for Medical Education and Research. "Retinal Detachment." Mayo Clinic, August 28, 2020. https://www.mayoclinic.org/diseases-conditions/retinal-detachment/symptoms-causes/syc-20351344.

Rindermann, Heiner, A. Laura Ackermann, and Jan te Nijenhuis. "Does Blindness Boost Working Memory? A Natural Experiment and Cross-Cultural Study." Frontiers, June 11, 2020. https://www.frontiersin.org/articles/10.3389/fpsyg.2020.01571/full.

Röder B, F. Rösler, and H.J. Neville. "Auditory Memory in Congenitally Blind Adults: A Behavioral-Electrophysiological Investigation." Cognitive brain research 11, no. 2 (April 2001): 289-303. https://doi.org/10.1016/s0926-6410(01)00002-7.

## CHAPTER 9: CREATIVE PROBLEM-SOLVING

CareerBuilder. "What Are Problem-Solving Skills and Why Are They Important?" June 13, 2017. https://www.careerbuilder.com/advice/what-are-problem-solving-skills-and-why-are-they-important.

Doyle, Alison. "What Are Problem-Solving Skills?" The Balance Careers, October 21, 2020. https://www.thebalancecareers.com/problem-solving-skills-with-examples-2063764.

Engler, Scott. "The Talent Angle with Scott Engler: Removing Barriers to Accessibility with Anil Lewis on Apple Podcasts." Apple Podcasts, November 24, 2020. Audio, 35:19. https://podcasts.apple.com/us/podcast/the-talent-angle-with-scott-engler/id1066056346?i=1000500056834.

Harris, Alexander. "5 US Cities With the Best Public Transportation." MYMOVE, January 13, 2021. https://www.mymove.com/city-guides/compare/best-public-transportation/.

National Center for Health Research. "Blind Adults in America: Their Lives and Challenges." January 22, 2018. https://www.center4research.org/blind-adults-america-lives-challenges/.

## CHAPTER 10: MOTIVATION

Barrett-Poindexter, Jacqui. "Busting the Myths around Workers with Disabilities." Lever (blog). October 1, 2019. https://www.lever.co/blog/busting-the-myths-around-workers-with-disabilities/.

Perkbox. "Why Employee Motivation Is Important & How to Improve It." Accessed June 11, 2021. https://www.perkbox.com/uk/resources/blog/why-employee-motivation-is-important-and-how-to-improve-measure-and-maintain-it.

R, Heryati. "Why Employee Motivation Is Important (& How to Improve It)." The 6Q Blog, August 26, 2019. https://inside.6q.io/employee-motivation-important/.

Romeo, Marina & Yepes-Baldó, Montserrat. (2019). Future Work and Disability: Promoting Job Motivation in Special Employment Centers in Spain. International Journal of Environmental Research and Public Health. 16. 1447. 10.3390/ijerph16081447.

The American Foundation for the Blind. "Key Employment Statistics." Accessed September 23, 2021. https://www.afb.org/research-and-initiatives/statistics/archived-statistics/key-employment-statistics.

US National Library of Medicine. "Leber Congenital Amaurosis: MedlinePlus Genetics." MedlinePlus, August 18, 2020. https://medlineplus.gov/genetics/condition/leber-congenital-amaurosis/#:~:text=Description,visual%20impairment%20beginning%20in%20infancy.

Virginia Commonwealth University. "The Realities of Hiring People with Disabilities Fact Sheet." VCU RRTC. Accessed May 23, 2021.
https://vcurrtc.org/resources/viewContent.cfm/589.


## CHAPTER 11: EDUCATING YOURSELF

American Foundation for the Blind. "Key Employment Statistics for People Who Are Blind or Visually Impaired." December 2014.
https://www.afb.org/research-and-initiatives/statistics/archived-statistics/key-employment-statistics.

Eye Health Observances - American Academy of Ophthalmology. "Eye Health Observances." Accessed September 23, 2021. https://www.aao.org/newsroom/observances.

National Industries for the Blind. "National Survey Reveals Increased Awareness About the Capabilities of People Who Are Blind in the Workforce." March 2, 2019. Accessed June 13,2021.
https://www.nib.org/press/national-survey-reveals-increased-awareness-about-the-capabilities-of-people-who-are-blind-in-the-workforce/.

US Census Bureau. "National Disability Employment Awareness Month: October 2021," September 23, 2021.
https://www.census.gov/newsroom/stories/disability-employment-awareness-month.html#:~:text=From%20the%20US%20Department%20of,of%20America's%20workers%20with%20disabilities.%E2%80%9D

The Chicago Lighthouse. "Employment & Training." Accessed June 19, 2021. https://chicagolighthouse.org/programs-services/employment-training/.

"What Is White Cane Day?" Accessed September 23, 2021. https://whitecaneday.org/.

**CHAPTER 12: HOW TO LEVERAGE STATE RESOURCES**

American Association of People with Disabilities, and Disability:IN. "Getting to Equal: The Disability Inclusion … - Accenture.com." Accenture. Accessed October 12, 2021. https://www.accenture.com/_acnmedia/PDF-89/Accenture-Disability-Inclusion-Research-Report.pdf].

Associated Press. "Many Employers Still Reluctant to Hire Blind Workers ." Daily News, November 4, 2013. https://www.nydailynews.com/life-style/health/employers-reluctant-hire-blind-workers-article-1.1506358.

Bureau of Services for the Visually Impaired. "Services for the Visually Impaired." Opportunities for Ohioans with Disabilities. Accessed July 6, 2021. https://ood.ohio.gov/wps/portal/gov/ood/individuals-with-disabilities/services/services-for-the-visually-impaired.

Division of Vocational Rehabilitation Florida Department of Education. "Employers." Vocational Rehabilitation Employer Page. Accessed September 23, 2021. http://www.rehabworks.org/employers.shtml.

Smith, J.D., Allen. "Can People with Disabilities Use Your Careers Website?" SHRM, October 22, 2018. https://www.shrm.org/resourcesandtools/legal-and-compliance/employment-law/pages/can-people-with-disabilities-use-your-careers-website.aspx.

## CHAPTER 13: CREATING ACCESSIBLE APPLICATIONS AND INTERVIEWS

Office of Disability Employment Policy. "Focus on Ability: Interviewing Applicants with Disabilities." United States Department of Labor. Accessed July 21, 2021. https://www.dol.gov/agencies/odep/publications/fact-sheets/focus-on-ability-interviewing-applicants-with-disabilities.

Saunderson, Roy. "Top 10 Ways Hiring Disabled Workers Can Motivate All." Northstar Meetings Group. October 7, 2010. https://www.northstarmeetingsgroup.com/Incentive/Strategy/Top-10-Ways-Hiring-Disabled-Workers-Can-Motivate-All.

Smith, J.D., Allen. "Can People with Disabilities Use Your Careers Website?" SHRM, October 22, 2018. https://www.shrm.org/resourcesandtools/legal-and-compliance/employment-law/pages/can-people-with-disabilities-use-your-careers-website.aspx.

## CHAPTER 14: EMPOWERING DIVERSITY AND INCLUSION

Casey, Caroline. "Do Your d&i Efforts Include People with Disabilities?" Harvard Business Review, March 19, 2020. https://hbr.org/2020/03/do-your-di-efforts-include-people-with-disabilities.

Jensen, Alexander. "How to Make Your Workplace More Inclusive for Visually Impaired Employees." Be My Eyes - See the world together. Be My Eyes2008, October 8, 2020. https://www.bemyeyes.com/blog/how-to-make-your-workplace-more-inclusive-for-visually-impaired-employees.

Lorenzo, Roci'o, Nicole Voigt, Miki Tsusaka, Matt Krentz, and Katie Abouzahr. "How Diverse Leadership Teams Boost Innovation." BCG. Boston Consulting Group, May 25, 2021. https://www.bcg.com/en-us/publications/2018/how-diverse-leadership-teams-boost-innovation.

Maurer, Roy. "Recruiting and Retaining People with Disabilities." SHRM, February 9, 2015. https://www.shrm.org/resourcesandtools/hr-topics/talent-acquisition/pages/recruiting-retaining-people-disabilities.aspx.

Miller, Bridget. "Can Employers Require Employees to Have Driver's Licenses?" HR Daily Advisor, September 10, 2020. https://hrdailyadvisor.blr.com/2020/09/15/can-employers-require-employees-to-have-drivers-licenses/.

Mondal, Somen. "Diversity and Inclusion: A Complete Guide for HR Professionals." Ideal (blog), September 15, 2021. https://ideal.com/diversity-and-inclusion/.

Rosen, Peg. "8 Inclusive Ways to Rethink Your Interview Strategy for People with Disabilities." Understood, May 4, 2021. https://www.understood.org/articles/en/8-inclusive-ways-to-rethink-your-interview-strategy-for-people-with-disabilities.

The American Foundation for the Blind. "Disability Employment RESEARCH: Key Takeaways." Accessed August 1, 2021. https://www.afb.org/research-and-initiatives/employment/reviewing-disability-employment-research-people-blind-visually.

Made in the USA
Monee, IL
05 March 2024

54491598R00105